Grow Where You Are

*Patio, Balcony & Countertop
Gardening for Real Life*

Ashley M. King

Grow Where You Are: *Patio, Balcony & Countertop Gardening for Real Life*

Copyright 2026 By Ashley M. King

All rights reserved. No part of this book may be used or reproduced, stored in a retrieval system, or transmitted in any form or in any manner whatsoever without written permission except in the case of brief quotations embodied in critical articles or reviews.

Published by Get It Done Publishing
Atlanta, GA 30349
www.getitdonepublishing.com
Printed in the United States of America
Paperback ISBN: 978-1-952561-46-7
Ebook ISBN: 978-1-952561-47-4
Library of Congress Control Number: 2026902039

Table of Contents

You Don't Need a Yard to Grow	8
Understanding Your Space	11
Light — The Make-or-Break Factor	19
Choosing the Right Containers	29
Soil Simplified	39
What to Grow and What to Skip	45
Planting for Success	55
Watering Without Fear	61
Feeding Container Plants	69
Growing Methods You Might See Online	77
Flowers, Fruit, and Productivity	85
Pests & Problems Without Panic	93
Seasonal Care & Long-Term Success	101
Making Gardening Fit Your Life	109
Growing Confidence, Not Just Plants	115
Resources	119

Author's Note

Listen, sis — I didn't learn how to garden by getting everything right the first time.

Let me tell you, I learned by trying, failing, adjusting, and trying again. I learned by killing plants, asking questions, and paying attention to what worked and what didn't. Over time — with patience and a little knowledge — things started to make sense.

That's the spirit behind this book.

You don't need perfection to grow plants. You need curiosity, observation, and a willingness to learn as you go. Mistakes aren't failures here — they're information. Every plant teaches you something if you let it.

This book was written to meet you where you are, not where you think you should be. Take what works, skip what doesn't, and trust that learning by doing is not only enough — it's often the best way forward.

Your Big Sis in the Garden,

-Ashley King

You Don't Need a Yard to Grow

You Don't Need a Yard to Grow

If you've ever stood in the produce section at the store and thought, *"I could grow this,"* but then immediately followed it up with *"Yeah, but not where I live,"* — girl, you're not alone.

Somewhere along the way, we picked up the idea that gardening requires a yard, raised beds, and more space than most of us actually have. And chile, listen — that belief has stopped a lot of perfectly capable people from ever trying.

The truth is simple: you don't need a yard to grow food, enjoy plants, or build confidence as a gardener. You just need a small space, a little patience, and some guidance that actually makes sense.

Let Me Be Honest for a Moment

I didn't start out good at this.

In fact, I had what I proudly called a *black thumb*. I killed plants with confidence. Herbs, flowers, vegetables — if it was green and living, I somehow found a way to take it out. I watered too much, didn't water enough, picked the wrong containers, used the wrong soil, and expected plants to just *figure it out*.

They did not.

What changed wasn't talent. It was understanding. Once I learned why plants struggled — especially in containers — things started to click. I didn't become perfect overnight, but over time, with patience and a little knowledge, I got better. And more importantly, I stopped being afraid to try.

That's the place this book comes from.

Why Small-Space Gardening Actually Works

Plants don't care about square footage. They care about conditions.

When you grow in containers — on a patio, balcony, porch, or even a sunny countertop — you actually gain more control, not less. You choose the soil. You decide where the plant sits. You can move it, adjust it, and respond to what it's telling you.

For beginners, apartment dwellers, and seniors especially, that control makes all the difference. You're not fighting poor ground soil, guessing where water drains, or dealing with a space you can't manage. You're working with a system that fits your life.

Let's Reset Expectations

This kind of gardening isn't about replacing your entire grocery run. It's about small wins that add up.

A handful of fresh herbs.
A bowl of greens you cut yourself.
A tomato that ripened right outside your door.

Those moments matter. They build confidence. They remind you that you *can* do this. And for many people, that confidence spills into other areas of life too.

If You've Tried Before and It Didn't Work

If you're coming into this with a little side-eye because you've tried before and failed — leave that attitude at the door but know that you're in good company.

Most people don't fail because they lack ability. They fail because no one explained how containers behave differently than the ground, or how light really works indoors, or why watering advice always seems to contradict itself.

This book doesn't just tell you *what* to do. It explains the *why*, so when something goes wrong — and sometimes it will — you're not stuck guessing.

Who This Book Is For

This book is for you if you:

- live in an apartment, condo, or townhome
- have a patio, balcony, porch, or sunny window
- want simple systems, not complicated rules
- kill plants and want to prove otherwise

You don't need fancy tools. You don't need a perfect setup. And you definitely don't need a yard.

How to Use This Book

You can read this book from start to finish, or jump straight to the chapters that matter most to you right now. Each section stands on its own, but together they give you a clear, realistic path forward.

Along the way, you'll find:

- plain-language explanations
- step-by-step guidance
- photos and diagrams to make things click
- checklists to simplify decisions
- tips that work for real life, not just ideal conditions

Before We Get Started

Gardening doesn't require perfection. Plants grow in imperfect conditions all the time. What matters is starting, paying attention, and being willing to adjust. Start where you are, use what you have, and grow from there.

CHAPTER 01

Understanding Your Space

Understanding Your Space

Before you buy a pot, a plant, or a bag of soil, you need to understand one thing first: your space determines your strategy.

Not Pinterest.
Not Instagram.
Not what worked for somebody with a backyard three states away.

Your space.

Once you understand what you're working with, everything else gets easier — and a whole lot less frustrating.

Start With the Space You Actually Have

When people say, *"I don't have space to garden,"* what they usually mean is, *"I don't have the space I imagine gardening requires."*

I used to think the same way.

When I first started growing anything, I didn't begin with a yard or a beautiful setup. I started with whatever space I had at the time — and chile, it was not ideal. I put plants where I *thought* they should go instead of where they actually worked. Too much shade. Too much heat. Too much guessing.

And when things died (because they did), I blamed myself instead of the setup.

What I learned over time is this: most "black thumb" stories are really space misunderstandings.

Once I slowed down and paid attention to where plants actually did well — not where I wished they would — everything started to change.

You Don't Need More Space — You Need the Right Spot

You don't need:

- a yard
- raised beds
- fancy structures
- or a perfect outdoor area

You do need:

- a spot that gets light
- enough room for a container
- a place that fits your daily routine

That might be:

- a patio or porch
- a balcony
- a railing
- a front stoop
- a sunny window
- a kitchen counter near natural light

If you can set a cup down there without knocking it over, you can probably grow something there.

Patio, Balcony, or Porch Gardening

Outdoor small spaces give you flexibility, but they also come with realities people don't always think about at first.

Things to Pay Attention To

- sun exposure: morning vs afternoon sun matters
- wind: especially on balconies and upper levels
- heat: concrete and brick hold heat longer
- water runoff: where does excess water go?
- weight limits: especially important for balconies

Chile, listen — if your space feels uncomfortable for *you* in the middle of summer, it probably feels that way for your plants too.

Best Uses for Outdoor Spaces

- tomatoes and peppers
- greens and herbs
- strawberries
- flowers for pollinators
- dwarf or patio fruit varieties

Countertop & Indoor Growing

Indoor growing works beautifully — when expectations are realistic. Indoor plants rely on light, consistency, and restraint. This is not the place to try to grow everything at once.

Great Indoor Candidates

- herbs (basil, parsley, mint, thyme)
- microgreens
- lettuce and baby greens
- green onions
- small flowering plants

Indoor plants usually grow slower, need more consistent care, and don't forgive overwatering as easily. One or two well-placed plants will build more confidence than five struggling ones spread around the house.

Please note that some plants can work in multiply spaces, but you'll need to adjust accordingly.

Choose Your Primary Growing Zones

Instead of trying to grow everywhere, choose one or two main spots and focus there.

Ask yourself:

- where do I already spend time?
- where will I actually remember to water?
- where won't plants be in the way?
- where can I easily see how they're doing?

Your best growing space is the one you won't forget about. Trust me. I've grown some things, forgot about them, and it wasn't until weeks later, when I was walking by that I realized it's now dead.

A Quick Exercise: Find Your First Spot

Before moving on, pause here for a moment. Think of one place in your home or outdoor area that:

- gets light
- is easy to access
- fits your daily routine

That's it. One spot.

You can always expand later. Right now, we're building confidence — not a full garden.

If you'd like help thinking this through on paper, you'll find a Space Assessment Worksheet in the Resources section at the back of this book.

Accessibility & Lifestyle Matters (Especially Long-Term)

Your garden should fit your life, not create more work. If bending, lifting, or carrying water is difficult:

- choose waist-high surfaces
- use lighter containers
- keep plants close to water sources

If memory or energy is limited:

- grow fewer plants
- place them where you'll see them daily
- stick to simple routines

Plants do better when *you* are comfortable caring for them.

Light Comes Next (But Don't Stress Yet)

For now, just notice:

- which areas get direct sunlight?
- how long that light lasts?
- what time of day it shows up?

Don't overthink it yet. Observation comes before action. We'll break light down clearly in the next chapter.

Common Mistakes at This Stage

Let's save you some frustration:

- buying plants before choosing a spot
- overestimating how much space you want to manage
- copying setups that don't match your light
- ignoring wind, heat, or access
- trying to grow too many things at once

Starting small isn't playing it safe — it's playing it smart.

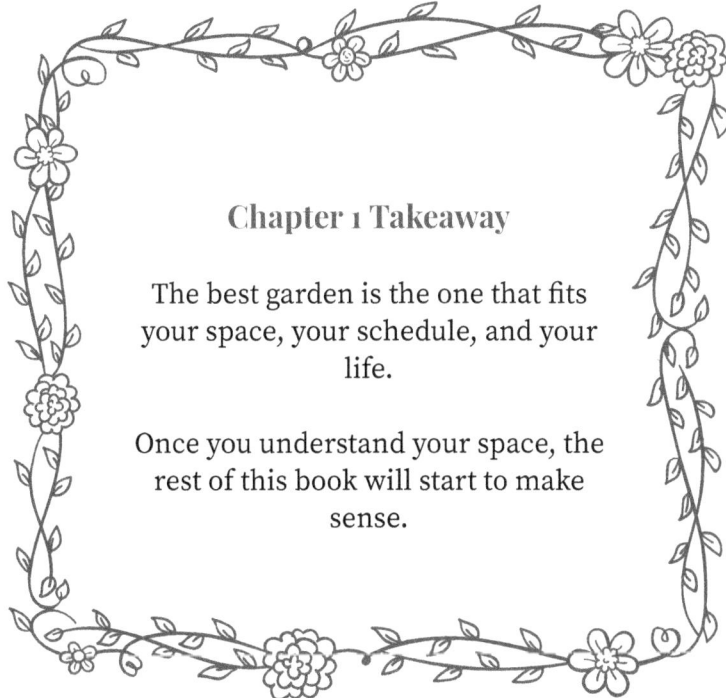

Chapter 1 Takeaway

The best garden is the one that fits your space, your schedule, and your life.

Once you understand your space, the rest of this book will start to make sense.

CHAPTER

Light — The Make-or-Break Factor

Light —
The Make-or-Break Factor

If there's one thing that determines whether plants simply survive or actually thrive, it's light.

Not soil.
Not fertilizer.
Not how often you talk to them.

Light.

And this is where a lot of people get tripped up — not because they aren't trying, but because light is often explained in a way that feels vague, technical, or downright confusing.

Let's clear that up.

What "Full Sun" Really Means (In Real Life)

When plant labels say *full sun*, they're not talking about brightness or warmth. They're talking about time.

Full sun means:

- 6–8 hours of direct sunlight per day

Partial sun or partial shade usually means:

- 4–6 hours of direct sunlight

Shade means:

- less than 4 hours of direct sunlight

This is important because a bright space is not always a sunny space. A room can feel well-lit to you and still not provide enough light for certain plants.

Grow Where You Are

Direct Light vs Bright Light

This is one of the most misunderstood parts of indoor growing.

- direct light means sunlight hits the plant directly.

Examples:

- sunbeams on a balcony plant
- a windowsill where sunlight lands on the plant
- patio containers in open sun

This is what plants use to make food through photosynthesis.

- bright light means the space feels light to *you*, but the sun doesn't actually hit the plant.

Examples:

- light through a window but not touching the plant
- a room that feels sunny but the plant is several feet away
- light filtered by curtains, trees, or buildings

Bright light does not count toward sunlight hours for most plants. Many houseplants tolerate bright light. Most food plants do not.

Bright light is well-lit but indirect. Direct light has sunbeams that physically hit the plant leaves.

If your plant isn't producing, stretching toward the window, or staying small and pale, light is often the reason.

Understanding Window Direction (Without Overthinking It)

Here's a simple way to think about windows:

- **South-facing windows**
  Most consistent light throughout the day. Best for indoor food plants.

- **East-facing windows**
  Gentle morning sun. Good for herbs and leafy greens.

- **West-facing windows**
  Strong afternoon sun. Can be great, but watch for heat stress.

- **North-facing windows**
  Lowest light. Best for decorative plants, not most edibles.

If you don't know which direction your window faces, that's okay. Observation will tell you more than labels ever will. And if you really want to be sure, a simple compass works — or chile, download a free compass app on your phone. That's what I use. Technology can help us garden too.

Outdoor Light Is Different Than Indoor Light

This part matters.

Outdoor light is stronger, even on cloudy days. That's why patios, balconies, and porches often allow more flexibility with plant choices than indoor spaces.

However, outdoor light comes with variables:

- seasonal changes
- shadows from buildings or railings
- trees and overhangs
- heat reflecting off concrete or walls

That's why noticing patterns over a few days is more helpful than guessing once.

A Simple Way to Observe Your Light

Before moving plants around or buying new ones, take a few days to notice:

- when does the sun first hit this space?
- how long does it stay?
- does the light move or disappear suddenly?
- is it filtered or direct?

You don't need exact hours. You just need a general sense. Light patterns will guide better decisions than any plant tag ever could. If you want to put this into practice, there's a Light Observation Worksheet in the Resources section at the back of this book to help you track what you're seeing over a few days.

When Grow Lights Make Sense (And When They Don't)

Grow lights aren't cheating. They're tools. They're especially helpful if:

- you want to grow indoors year-round
- your windows don't provide enough direct sun
- you're growing herbs, greens, or seedlings
- winter light is limited

You don't need an expensive setup. A simple light used consistently works better than a powerful light used randomly.

What matters most:

- distance from the plant
- consistent daily use
- matching the light to the plant's needs

The Kind of Light Vegetables Actually Need

Vegetables don't just need light — they need the right kind of light.

Think of light like food.
Not all food feeds your body the same way.
And not all light feeds plants the same way either.

A bright room might feel good to *you*, but vegetables need light that actually supports growth.

Here's what vegetables care about most.

Bright, Strong Light

Vegetables need stronger light than most houseplants.

Herbs, lettuce, tomatoes, and peppers grow best when the light is bright enough to cast a clear shadow. If your light is soft and dim, plants may stay alive — but they usually won't grow well.

Sis, listen — surviving is not the same as thriving.

Light That Stays Close

Grow lights work best when they're close to the plant — usually 6–12 inches away.

If the light is too far away, it becomes weak, even if it looks bright to your eyes. Light strength drops quickly with distance.

Closer light = stronger light for the plant.

Enough Hours of Light

Most vegetables need:

- 12–16 hours of light per day
- darkness at night to rest

Plants respond best to light that's consistent, not random. Turning a light on and off whenever you remember doesn't give plants what they need to grow steadily.

Light Made for Growing Plants

When choosing a light for vegetables, look for labels that say:

- drow light
- full spectrum
- for plants or seedlings

You don't need to understand the science behind it. Just remember this:

Regular lamps are made for people. Grow lights are made for plants.

Big Sis Truth

A room can look bright and still not give plants what they need. Plants need strong, direct light — not just light that looks good to us. And more hours of weak light won't make up for light that isn't strong enough.

Vegetables grow best with bright, close, consistent plant light — and once that's in place, everything else gets easier.

Signs Your Plant Isn't Getting Enough Light

Plants are good communicators if you know what to look for.

Common signs include:

- long, leggy growth
- leaning or stretching toward the light
- pale or yellowing leaves
- little to no flowering or fruit
- slow growth despite proper care

If you see these signs, don't panic. Light can often be adjusted without starting over.

Too Much Light Is Also a Thing

Especially outdoors or in strong west-facing windows.

Signs of too much light include:

- scorched or bleached leaves
- crispy edges
- wilting even when soil is moist
- plants looking stressed in the afternoon

Sometimes the fix is as simple as:

- moving the plant a few inches
- adding light shade
- changing the time of exposure

Match the Plant to the Light (Not the Other Way Around)

This one shift saves people a lot of frustration. Instead of asking, *"How do I make this plant work here?"* Ask, *"What plants work well in this light?"*

Low-light spaces can still grow:

- herbs like mint and parsley
- leafy greens
- decorative plants

High-light spaces can handle:

- tomatoes and peppers
- basil
- strawberries
- flowering plants

Let the light choose the plant.

Common Light Mistakes

Let's call them out:

- assuming bright rooms equal enough light
- moving plants too often without observing
- expecting indoor plants to perform like outdoor ones
- ignoring seasonal light changes
- overcompensating with water or fertilizer instead of adjusting light

Light problems often look like watering problems — until you know better.

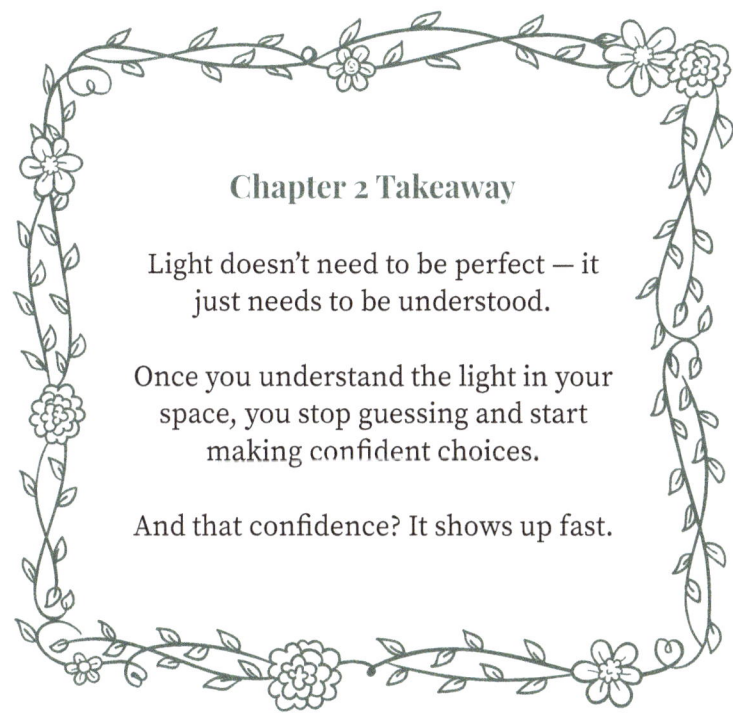

Chapter 2 Takeaway

Light doesn't need to be perfect — it just needs to be understood.

Once you understand the light in your space, you stop guessing and start making confident choices.

And that confidence? It shows up fast.

CHAPTER 03

Choosing the Right Containers

Choosing the Right Containers

Let's talk about containers — because the pot you choose matters more than most people realize. A lot of folks pick containers based on looks first. And listen, there's nothing wrong with wanting things to be cute. But when the container doesn't meet the plant's needs, no amount of sunshine or good intentions can save it.

The good news? Once you understand a few basics, choosing containers becomes simple instead of stressful.

Why the Container Matters So Much

When you grow in the ground, roots can spread out, search for water, and adjust to changes. In a container, roots are limited to what you give them.

That means the container controls:

- how much water the plant can hold
- how quickly soil dries out
- how warm the roots get
- how much room roots have to grow

In other words, the container is the plant's entire world.

Size Matters (More Than Shape)

One of the most common beginner mistakes is choosing a container that's too small.

Small pots:

- dry out quickly
- require more frequent watering
- limit root growth
- tip over easily

Larger containers:

- hold moisture longer
- support healthier root systems
- need less frequent watering
- offer more forgiveness if you miss a day

As a general rule: When in doubt, go bigger.

It's much easier to manage one slightly oversized container than to babysit a pot that's too small.

Depth vs Width: What Plants Actually Need

Different plants care about different dimensions.

- deep containers are best for:
    - tomatoes
    - peppers
    - root vegetables
    - fruit plants
- wider containers work well for:
    - herbs
    - lettuce and greens
    - flowers
    - mixed plantings

Drainage: Non-Negotiable

Let's be very clear here:

Plants in containers need drainage holes. Without drainage:

- roots sit in water
- soil stays soggy
- roots suffocate and rot

If your container doesn't have holes, you have three options:

1. Drill drainage holes (if the material allows)

2. Use the container as a decorative cover and place a pot with holes inside

3. Choose a different container

Putting rocks in the bottom does not fix drainage problems. It actually makes them worse.

Do Rocks at the Bottom of Pots Really Help with Drainage?

Chile… this one comes up *all the time.*

If you've ever been told to put rocks or gravel in the bottom of a pot "for drainage," you are not wrong for believing it. Girl, listen — I was told the same thing. When I was first learning, someone encouraged me to put rocks at the bottom of a plant, and of course I did. I was trying to do things right, and that advice sounded logical.

Here's what actually happens in a container. When you put rocks in the bottom of a pot, water doesn't drain the way we expect. Here's a better way to picture what's actually happening.

Think of your soil like a wet sponge, and the rocks like marbles sitting underneath it. When you pour water onto a sponge, it doesn't immediately let go just because there's space below it. The sponge holds onto water. It has to get *very* wet before any water drips down into the marbles.

That's exactly what happens in a pot. The soil holds onto water first. Only once it's fully saturated does extra water move down past the soil and into the rock layer. By that point, the soil where the roots live is already too wet — and that's where problems start.

So even though water eventually collects at the bottom of the pot, the issue happens *before* that. The root zone stays soggy longer than it should, and roots don't love that.

Instead of helping drainage, rocks often lead to:

- water sitting higher in the pot
- roots staying too wet
- increased risk of root rot
- plants wilting even though the soil is damp

That's why a plant can look like it needs water… when it actually has too much.

So why do so many people swear by this method? Because rocks *do* help with drainage in the ground and in large outdoor systems where water can keep moving downward. Containers are different. They're a closed system. Once water hits the bottom, it can't go anywhere except out the drainage hole — and the soil above controls how fast that happens.

Now, there *are* a couple situations where people use rocks in containers — but let's be clear about what they're really doing.

Rocks can help:

- add weight to tall or top-heavy containers so they don't tip over
- provide stability in windy areas like balconies
- sit below a barrier (like mesh or a broken pottery shard) to keep soil from washing out

In these cases, rocks are helping with stability, not drainage.

What actually improves drainage and overall plant health is much simpler:

- using a quality potting mix made for containers
- choosing containers with proper drainage holes
- avoiding compacted or heavy soil
- giving roots enough room to grow

Healthy drainage comes from soil structure, not what's sitting at the bottom of the pot.

And if you've used rocks before, don't beat yourself up. Most of us learned that advice from someone who meant well. Gardening is full of things that sound right until you understand what's really happening under the surface. Once you know better, you do better — and your plants absolutely notice the difference.

Container Materials: Pros and Cons

Not all containers behave the same way.

Plastic & Resin

- lightweight
- holds moisture well
- good for balconies and indoor use
- can heat up in direct sun

Terracotta & Clay

- breathable
- helps prevent overwatering
- dries out faster
- heavier and breakable

Ceramic

- attractive
- often heavy
- must have drainage holes

Wood

- insulates roots
- natural look
- needs lining to prevent rot

Fabric Grow Bags

- excellent drainage
- lightweight
- great for root health
- dry out faster

There's no "best" container — only what works best for your space, your plant, and your routine.

Weight, Stability, and Safety

This matters more than people expect.

Before placing a container, ask:

- can I lift this when it's full of soil and water?
- will it tip over in wind?
- is this safe for a balcony or railing?
- will water drip onto someone below?

If lifting is difficult:

- choose lighter materials
- use smaller containers
- place containers on rolling plant caddies
- keep them near water sources

Gardening should not strain your body.

How Many Plants Fit in One Container?

More plants does *not* equal more harvest.

Overcrowding leads to:

- competition for water and nutrients
- poor air circulation
- smaller harvests
- increased disease

Most plants do better with space to grow. One healthy plant often outperforms three struggling ones.

Later chapters will give you spacing guidance — for now, resist the urge to overfill.

Reusing Containers (Safely)

You don't need to buy everything new.

You can reuse:

- buckets
- storage bins
- old planters
- food-grade containers

Just make sure:

- they're clean
- they haven't held chemicals
- they have drainage holes

If it can safely hold soil, drain water, and stay stable, it can likely be used.

Accessibility & Ease of Care

Choose containers that make life easier, not harder.

Consider:

- waist-high planters to reduce bending
- lightweight materials
- containers you can easily move
- simple shapes that are easy to water

Plants thrive when care feels manageable. If you'd like help choosing containers that fit your space and lifestyle, you'll find a Container Selection Worksheet in the Resources section at the back of this book.

Common Container Mistakes

Let's save you some trouble:

- choosing containers that are too small
- ignoring drainage
- prioritizing looks over function
- overcrowding plants
- using containers that are hard to move or water

None of these mean you've failed — they just mean you're learning.

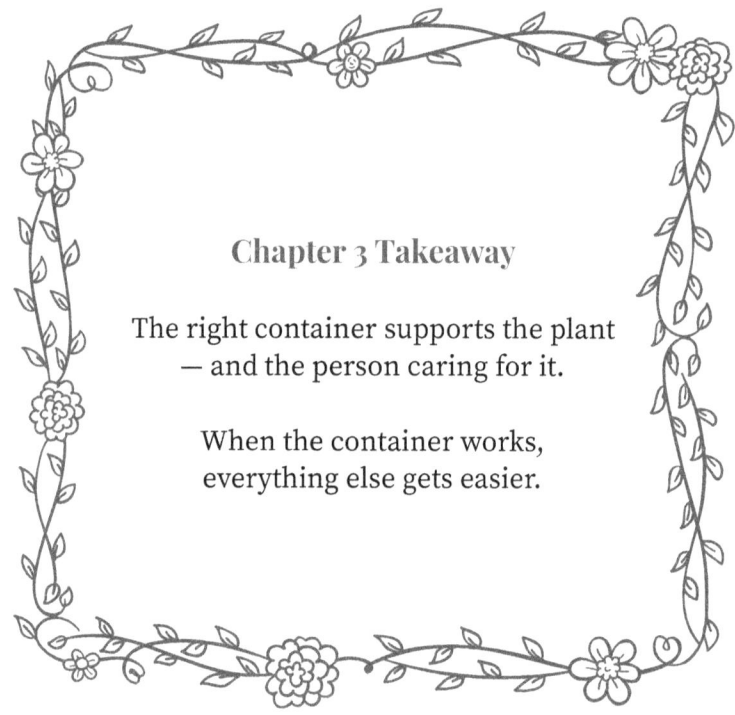

Chapter 3 Takeaway

The right container supports the plant — and the person caring for it.

When the container works, everything else gets easier.

CHAPTER 04

Soil Simplified

Soil Simplified

Let's clear something up right away: dirt and soil are not the same thing — especially in containers. And if that sentence alone makes you feel a little unsure, don't worry. This chapter exists so you don't have to guess, Google, or overthink what goes into your pots.

Because when soil is right, everything else gets easier.

Why Container Soil Is Different

When plants grow in the ground, soil has help. It's connected to a larger system that holds moisture, drains naturally, and balances itself over time. Containers don't have that luxury.

In a pot, soil has to:

- hold enough moisture for roots
- drain excess water
- allow air to reach roots
- stay loose over time
- support nutrients plants need

That's a lot to ask — which is why regular garden dirt doesn't work well in containers.

Why Garden Soil Is a No-Go in Pots

Chile, listen. I know it's tempting.

You see soil outside and think, *"Why buy potting mix when I already have dirt?"*

Been there. Done that. Learned the hard way.

Garden soil in containers:

- compacts easily
- drains poorly
- becomes heavy when wet
- limits airflow to roots
- can carry pests and disease

In the ground, those issues spread out. In a pot, they stack up — and plants suffer for it.

What "Potting Mix" Really Means

Potting mix isn't dirt. It's a blend designed specifically for containers.

Most quality potting mixes include:

- organic matter (like peat moss or coir) for moisture retention
- materials that create air pockets
- ingredients that help drainage
- sometimes a small amount of fertilizer

The goal isn't richness — it's balance.

If soil holds too much water, roots drown.
If it drains too fast, roots dry out.
Good potting mix finds the middle.

Peat, Coir, and What Those Words Mean

Let's demystify a few labels you'll see on bags.

- **Peat-based mixes**
  Hold moisture well and are very common. They need proper watering habits to avoid drying out too much.

- **Coir-based mixes**
  Made from coconut fibers. They hold moisture evenly and are often easier for beginners to manage.

Neither is "better" across the board. The best choice depends on:

- your climate
- how often you water
- whether plants are indoors or outdoors

Why Soil Changes Over Time

Soil doesn't stay the same forever — especially in containers.

Over time:

- organic matter breaks down
- air pockets disappear
- soil compacts
- drainage slows

That's why a pot that worked beautifully last season might struggle this season.

If water starts sitting on top or draining too slowly, the soil may need refreshing.

Reusing Soil (Without Causing Problems)

You don't need to throw soil away after one season — but you do need to be thoughtful.

You can reuse soil if:

- the previous plant was healthy
- there were no major pest or disease issues

Before reusing:

- remove old roots
- loosen the soil
- mix in fresh potting mix or compost

If plants struggled badly or disease was present, it's better to start fresh.

If you want help deciding whether to reuse, refresh, or replace your soil, you'll find a Soil Refresh Worksheet in the Resources section at the back of this book.

Common Soil Problems (And What They Usually Mean)

If you notice:

- water running straight through → soil may be too dry or broken down
- water sitting on top → soil may be compacted
- fungus gnats → soil staying too wet
- hard, crusty soil → organic matter depleted

These aren't failures. They're signals. Soil talks — you just have to learn how to listen.

For a quick reference when soil issues pop up, there's a Soil Troubleshooting Chart in the Resources section at the back of this book.

What Actually Improves Soil Performance

Instead of adding random materials, focus on:

- using quality potting mix
- choosing the right container size
- avoiding heavy garden soil
- refreshing soil as needed
- watering appropriately

Soil health is about structure, not shortcuts.

Accessibility & Simplicity Matter Here Too

If lifting heavy bags is difficult:

- look for lightweight potting mixes
- buy smaller bags
- ask for help loading — no shame in that

If remembering amendments feels overwhelming:

- choose mixes labeled "for containers"
- keep it simple
- consistency matters more than perfection

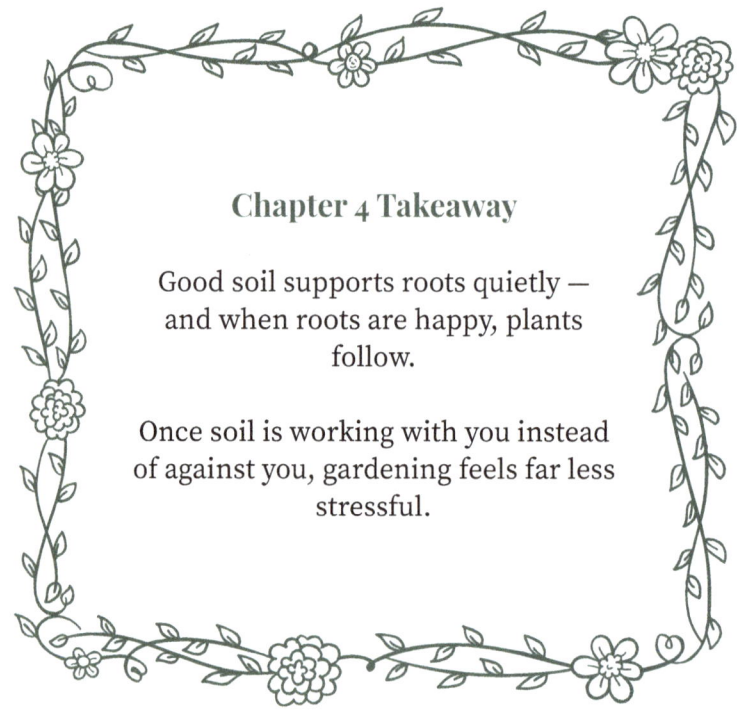

Chapter 4 Takeaway

Good soil supports roots quietly — and when roots are happy, plants follow.

Once soil is working with you instead of against you, gardening feels far less stressful.

CHAPTER 05

What to Grow and What to Skip

What to Grow and What to Skip

One of the fastest ways to lose confidence as a gardener is to start with the wrong plants. Not because you did anything wrong — but because no one told you that some plants are simply harder in containers, especially in small spaces. And chile, listen… struggling plants don't mean you're bad at gardening. They usually mean the plant and the setup weren't a good match.

This chapter is about setting you up for success from the very beginning.

Start with Wins, Not Wishes

It's tempting to grow what you *want* instead of what actually works well where you live. We've all done it. I sure have.

But confidence grows faster when:

- plants respond well to your care
- you see progress quickly
- you're not constantly troubleshooting

That's why starting with reliable plants matters — especially in containers.

Good, Better, Best: Choosing Plants That Match Your Experience

Let's take the pressure off for a moment.

Not every plant is meant to be your first plant. That doesn't mean you can't grow it — it just means timing matters. Think of this as levels, not labels. It's about what you're ready for right now — not what you're capable of forever.

Girl, listen… we all want to jump straight to the impressive stuff. Been there, done that. But confidence grows faster when you start with plants that actually want to grow where you live.

GOOD: Confidence Builders

Start here if you're new, busy, or want quick wins.

These plants tend to forgive mistakes and perform well in containers.

- basil
- mint
- parsley
- lettuce
- spinach
- green onions
- microgreens

Why these work:

- fast growth
- clear signs when they need care
- easy to harvest
- great for small spaces and indoors

If these do well, you're off to a strong start.

BETTER: Stepping Stones

Try these once you've had a few wins and understand your space.

- peppers
- strawberries
- bush or patio tomatoes
- mixed herb containers
- nasturtiums

These plants:

- need more consistent light
- benefit from regular feeding
- reward attention with bigger harvests

This is where many gardeners build confidence.

BEST: Challenge Plants (For Later)

Not bad plants — just demanding ones.

- large tomato varieties
- broccoli
- cauliflower
- corn
- pumpkins and melons
- root crops in shallow containers

These plants:

- need more space
- require deeper containers
- demand consistency
- can be frustrating early on

You can absolutely grow these — just don't let them be your first experience.

Big Sis Reminder

Skipping a plant isn't giving up. It's choosing progress. Start with Good, move into Better, and try Best when your space, time, and confidence line up. That's how gardeners grow.

The lists that follow help you match these experience levels to your actual space — indoors or outdoors.

Best Plants for Patios & Outdoor Containers

These plants tend to perform well in containers and forgive small mistakes.

Great Starter Choices

- herbs (basil, thyme, rosemary, mint, parsley)
- lettuce and leafy greens
- spinach and arugula
- strawberries
- peppers
- bush or patio tomatoes
- green onions

Why these work:

- compact growth
- manageable root systems
- clear signals when something's wrong
- high reward for relatively low effort

Best Plants for Countertops & Indoors

Indoor growing works best with plants that:

- don't require intense sunlight
- grow quickly
- are harvested regularly

Indoor-Friendly Options

- herbs (especially basil, parsley, mint)
- microgreens
- baby lettuce
- green onions (from kitchen scraps)
- small flowering plants

One or two thriving plants indoors will always beat a crowded collection of struggling ones.

Plants That Sound Easy (But Often Aren't)

Here's where honesty helps.

Some plants are often recommended to beginners but can be frustrating in containers.

Proceed with Caution

- large tomato varieties
- corn
- pumpkins and melons
- broccoli and cauliflower
- root vegetables in shallow containers

These plants need:

- deep soil
- consistent feeding
- strong light
- more space than most containers provide

You *can* grow them — but they're not the best confidence-builders early on.

Compact and Dwarf Varieties Are Your Friend

If you're growing in containers, variety choice matters just as much as the plant itself.

Look for words like:

- patio
- bush
- dwarf
- compact
- container-friendly

These varieties are bred to:

- stay smaller
- produce well in limited space
- handle container conditions better

How Much Can You Realistically Expect to Harvest?

Let's set expectations gently.

Container gardening:

- supplements your meals
- adds freshness and flavor
- builds confidence

It does not usually replace full grocery shopping.

A single tomato plant won't feed a family — but it *will* give you tomatoes you grew yourself. And that matters.

Mixing Plants in One Container (When It Works)

Mixed containers can be beautiful and productive — when plants share similar needs.

They work best with:

- herbs together
- lettuce and greens
- strawberries with shallow-rooted companions

Avoid mixing:

- fast growers with slow growers
- heavy feeders with light feeders
- sun lovers with shade lovers

When in doubt, fewer plants = fewer problems. For help deciding how many plants fit comfortably in one container, you'll find a Plant Spacing Guide in the Resources section at the back of this book.

Let the Space Choose the Plant

Instead of asking:

"What do I want to grow?"

Ask:

"What grows well in this space?"

Light, container size, and your routine should guide plant choices — not trends or wish lists. If you want help narrowing down what to grow based on your space and experience level, you'll find a Plant Selection Guide in the Resources section at the back of this book.

What to Skip (At Least for Now)

Skipping a plant is not quitting. It's strategy.

You might skip a plant because:

- it needs more space than you have
- it requires more time than you can give
- it doesn't match your light
- you want quicker wins first

You can always try it later — when your confidence and setup grow.

Common Plant Selection Mistakes

Let's save you some frustration:

- starting with too many plants
- choosing plants that outgrow containers quickly
- ignoring variety size
- mixing incompatible plants
- expecting indoor plants to perform like outdoor ones

Learning what *not* to grow is just as valuable as learning what to grow. Choose plants that work *with* your space and your life, not against them.

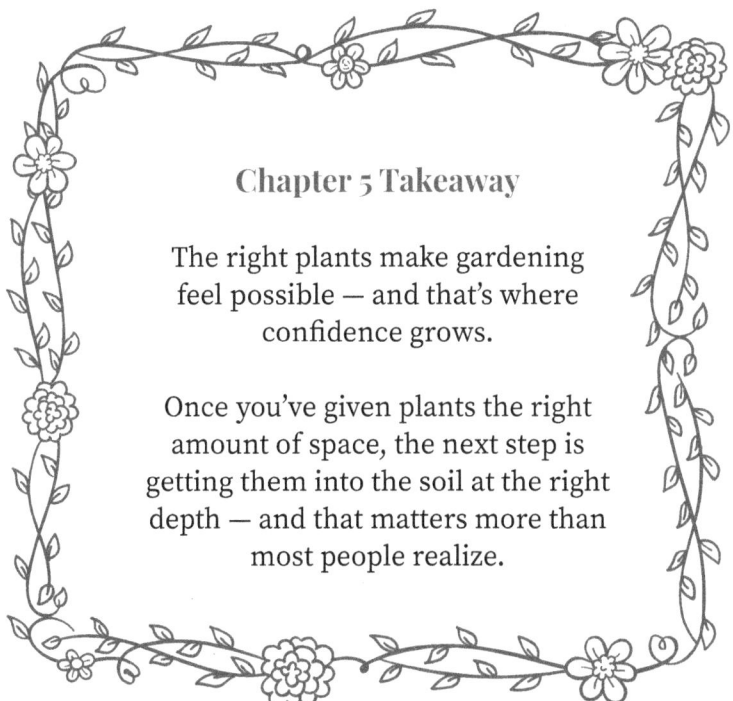

Chapter 5 Takeaway

The right plants make gardening feel possible — and that's where confidence grows.

Once you've given plants the right amount of space, the next step is getting them into the soil at the right depth — and that matters more than most people realize.

# CHAPTER 06

Planting for Success

Planting for Success

Planting is where a lot of people get nervous — not because it's hard, but because it feels final. Once the plant is in the pot, it can feel like there's no turning back.

Chile, listen… planting doesn't have to be perfect. It just needs to be thoughtful.

This chapter walks you through how to plant in containers the *right* way — without rushing, guessing, or overcomplicating things.

Before You Plant, Pause

Before soil ever goes into a pot, take a moment to check three things:

- you've chosen the right plant for your space
- you've given it enough room
- the container has drainage holes

If those are in place, you're already ahead of the game.

Step 1: Prepare the Container

Start with a clean container that has drainage holes.

If reusing a pot:

- remove old soil and debris
- rinse it out
- make sure holes aren't blocked

You don't need to disinfect unless there was disease before — simple and clean is enough.

Step 2: Add Soil (But Not All the Way Up)

Fill the container about two-thirds full with potting mix.

Why not fill it to the top?

- you need room to position the plant
- you want space for watering
- overfilled pots spill soil everywhere

Lightly loosen the soil with your hands. Don't pack it down — roots need air just as much as water.

Step 3: Remove the Plant Gently

Take the plant out of its nursery pot carefully.

If roots are tightly wound:

- gently loosen them with your fingers
- don't yank or tear
- just encourage them to spread

Been there, done that — rough handling slows plants down more than people realize. I'm guilty of man-handling plants so rough that I've broken a few, but don't tell anyone.

Step 4: Plant at the Right Depth

This part matters more than most folks think.

General rule:

- plant at the same depth it was growing before

Too shallow:

- roots dry out
- plant becomes unstable

Too deep:

- stems can rot
- growth slows

Exceptions exist (like tomatoes), but for most container plants, matching the original depth is best. For a quick reference on how deep common container plants should be planted, you'll find a Planting Depth Guide in the Resources section at the back of this book.

Step 5: Fill In and Settle the Soil

Add soil around the plant until it's supported but not buried.

Then:

- gently press the soil to remove air pockets
- don't compact it
- leave about an inch of space at the top for watering

That space matters more than it seems. This "headroom" helps prevent soil erosion and allows water to seep down evenly throughout the soil, all the way to the roots. Not to mention plant health, so that you can add mulch or even compost as the soil settles.

Step 6: Water Slowly and Thoroughly

After planting, water until you see water drain from the bottom.

This does two things:

- settles the soil
- helps roots make contact

Let excess water drain completely. Don't let pots sit in standing water unless the plant specifically needs it.

Spacing and Depth Work Together

Remember:

- proper spacing gives roots room
- proper depth helps roots anchor and absorb

Crowding and incorrect depth are two of the fastest ways to stress a plant early on.

If you're unsure how many plants belong in a container, refer back to the Plant Spacing Guide in the Resources section.

After Planting: What's Normal (And What's Not)

It's normal for plants to:

- look a little droopy for a day
- pause growth briefly
- adjust to their new home

Plant Shock Is Normal

Sis, listen — a little plant shock after planting is normal.

Plants don't always look happy right away after being moved. You might see some drooping, slowed growth, or leaves looking a little tired for a day or two. That doesn't mean you did anything wrong. It just means the plant is adjusting to new soil, new space, and new conditions.

Let me tell you something I had to learn the hard way: the worst thing you can do is panic and start fixing things that aren't broken. Give your plant time to settle in. Keep the soil evenly moist, leave it in one place, and resist the urge to fuss. Most plants bounce back once their roots get comfortable.

It's *not* normal for plants to:

- collapse completely
- turn yellow immediately
- sit in soggy soil for days

Most planting issues show up quickly — and most can be fixed just as quickly.

A Few Planting Mistakes to Avoid

Let's keep it real:

- planting too deep
- overpacking soil
- crowding plants
- forgetting to water after planting
- moving plants repeatedly right after planting

Once planted, give your plant a little time to settle in.

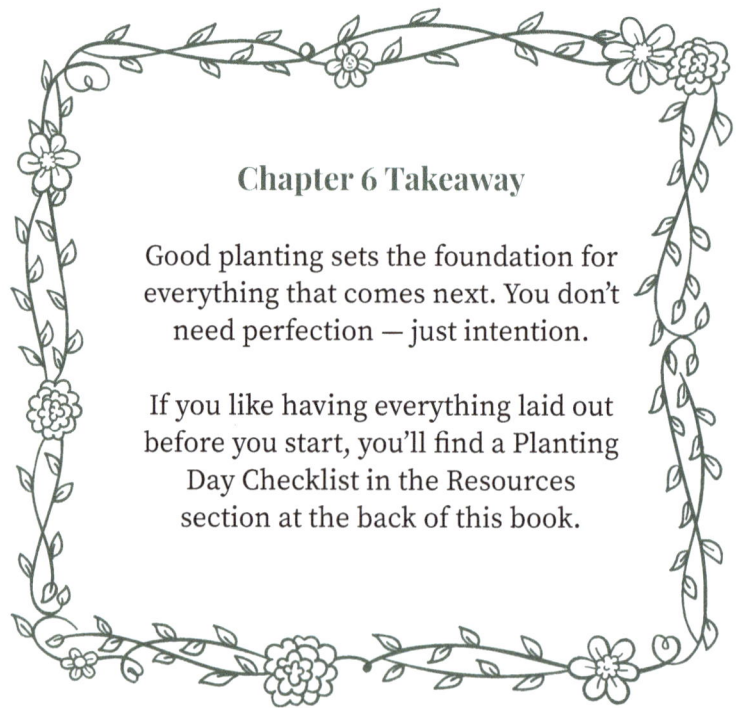

Chapter 6 Takeaway

Good planting sets the foundation for everything that comes next. You don't need perfection — just intention.

If you like having everything laid out before you start, you'll find a Planting Day Checklist in the Resources section at the back of this book.

CHAPTER 07

Watering Without Guessing

Watering Without Guessing

Watering feels like it should be simple — but somehow, it's where a lot of people get stuck. Too much? Too little? Morning or night? Every day or once a week? And why does the soil feel dry *and* soggy at the same time?

Listen, sis — watering isn't about a schedule. It's about paying attention. This chapter will help you stop guessing and start watering with confidence.

Why Watering Is Tricky in Containers

Containers behave differently than garden beds.

- they dry out faster
- they don't pull moisture from surrounding soil
- they rely completely on you

That doesn't mean they're hard — it just means watering needs to be intentional.

There Is No Perfect Watering Schedule

Let's clear this up right now.

There is no universal schedule that works for every plant, pot, or space.

Watering depends on:

- container size
- type of plant
- light exposure
- temperature
- wind
- time of year

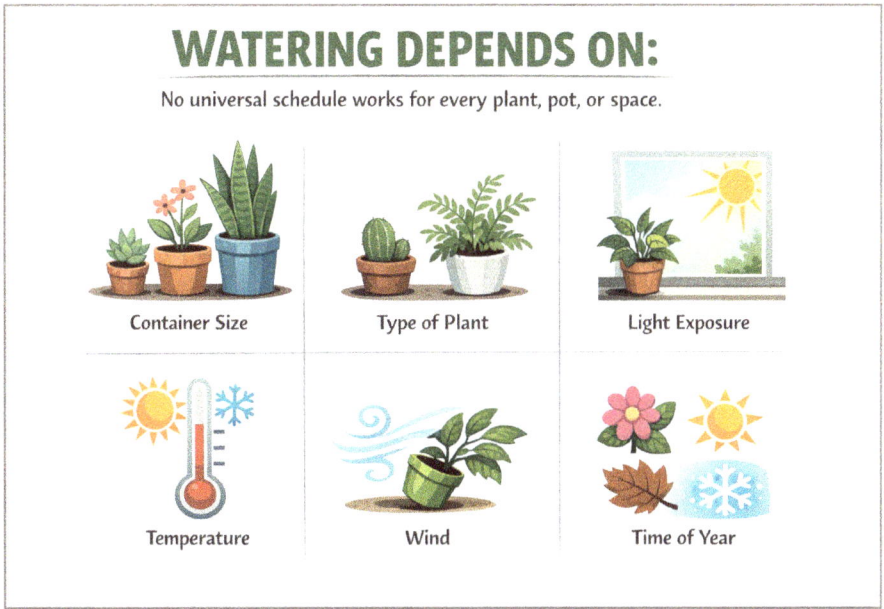

Anyone who tells you "water every two days" is oversimplifying. If you want help noticing patterns without locking yourself into a strict schedule, you'll find a Watering Rhythm Guide in the Resources section at the back of this book.

The Finger Test (Your Best Tool)

Forget fancy tools for now.

Your finger tells you more than a calendar ever will.

Here's how to check:

- stick your finger about 1–2 inches into the soil
- if it feels dry → water
- if it feels moist → wait

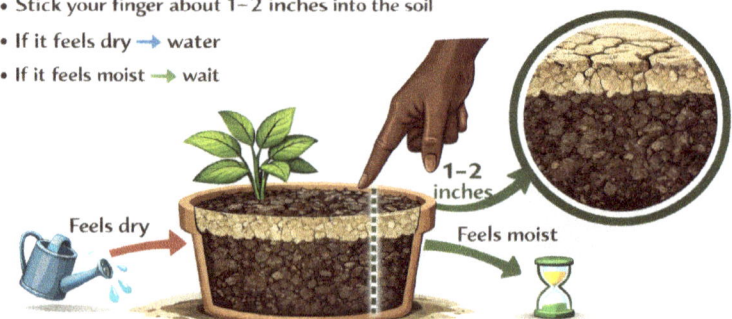

If the top looks dry but the soil underneath is still moist, don't water yet.

Been there, done that — watering too soon causes more problems than waiting a day.

Signs Your Plant Needs Water

Plants will tell you what they need if you know how to listen.

Common signs of thirst:

- wilting leaves
- dry soil
- lightweight containers
- leaves curling inward

Water slowly and deeply — not just a splash.

64

Drooping Isn't Always Thirst

Sis, drooping doesn't automatically mean your plant needs water.

Plants can droop when it's hot, after being moved, or while adjusting to new conditions. Sometimes they're protecting themselves, not crying out for help. Watering right away without checking the soil can do more harm than good.

Before you reach for the watering can, feel the soil. If it's still moist, give the plant some time. Many plants perk back up on their own once temperatures cool or stress passes.

Let the soil guide you — not just the leaves.

Signs You're Watering Too Much

Overwatering is one of the most common container mistakes.

Signs of too much water:

- yellowing leaves
- mushy stems
- soil that stays wet for days
- fungus gnats
- a sour smell from the soil

More water does not mean more care.

How to Water the Right Way

When you water, do it with intention.

- water slowly
- let water soak in
- stop when water drains from the bottom
- empty saucers if needed

Quick surface watering encourages shallow roots. Slow watering builds stronger plants.

Morning vs Evening Watering

Morning is best when possible.

Why:

- less evaporation
- plants are ready for the day
- leaves dry faster

Evening watering is okay if that's what works for your schedule — just avoid soaking leaves overnight when possible.

Indoor vs Outdoor Watering

Indoor plants:

- dry out slower
- need less frequent watering
- are more sensitive to overwatering

Outdoor containers:

- dry out faster
- need more frequent checks
- are affected by heat and wind

Same plant, different environment — different watering needs.

Newly Planted vs Established Plants

New plants:

- need consistent moisture
- should not dry out completely
- are more sensitive to stress

Established plants:

- can tolerate drying slightly between watering
- have stronger root systems

Watering needs change as plants grow.

What to Do When You're Not Sure

When in doubt:

- wait a day
- check the soil again
- observe the plant

Most plants recover from being a little dry faster than being drowned. Over time, combining gentle observation with a loose watering rhythm helps patterns become clear.

If keeping notes helps you notice those patterns faster, you'll find a Watering Log Worksheet in the Resources section at the back of this book.

Common Watering Mistakes to Avoid

Let's save you some trouble:

- watering on a strict schedule
- watering just the surface
- ignoring drainage
- letting pots sit in standing water
- panicking at the first droop

Patience matters here.

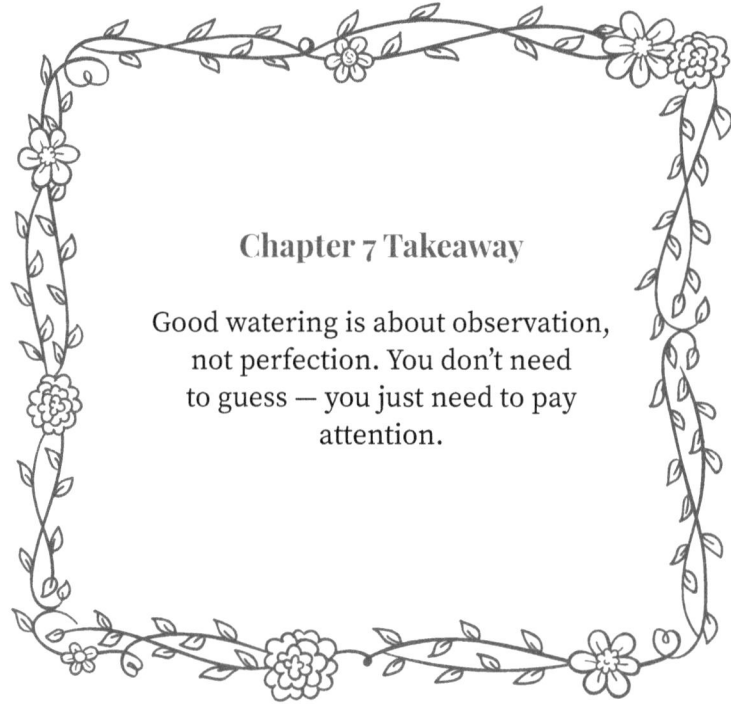

Chapter 7 Takeaway

Good watering is about observation, not perfection. You don't need to guess — you just need to pay attention.

CHAPTER 08

Feeding Your Plants Without Overdoing It

Feeding Your Plants Without Overdoing It

Feeding plants can feel intimidating. One aisle says "feeds instantly," another promises "explosive growth," and somewhere in between you're standing there thinking, *Lawd, which one do I pick?*

Listen — plants don't need gourmet meals. They need steady, sensible nourishment.

This chapter will help you understand when feeding helps, when it doesn't, and how to support your plants without overthinking or overdoing it.

Do Plants Always Need Fertilizer?

Short answer: no.

If you're using fresh potting mix, it already contains nutrients. Many plants grow just fine for weeks — sometimes months — without extra feeding.

Overfeeding causes more problems than underfeeding, especially in containers.

What Fertilizer Actually Does

Fertilizer doesn't make plants grow out of nowhere. It:

- replaces nutrients used up in containers
- supports leaf growth, root strength, and flowering
- helps plants recover from stress

Think of fertilizer as support, not a solution. For a simple overview of how and when to feed container plants, you'll find a Feeding Basics Guide in the Resources section at the back of this book.

When Feeding Is Helpful

Feeding can help when:

- plants have been growing for several weeks
- leaves look pale or growth has slowed
- plants are producing flowers or fruit
- containers have been watered often (nutrients wash out)

If your plant looks healthy and growing steadily, you may not need to feed yet. You'll find a Fertilizer Decision Chart in the Resources section at the back of this book, if you want help deciding whether feeding is necessary and what kind to use.

Signs You Might Need to Feed

Plants will give you clues.

Common signs include:

- pale or yellowing leaves (not caused by overwatering)
- slow growth
- smaller leaves
- reduced flowering or fruiting

Feeding should support recovery — not force growth.

Signs You're Feeding Too Much

Too much fertilizer can harm plants.

Watch for:

- burned or crispy leaf edges
- sudden leaf drop
- white crust on soil surface
- wilting even though soil is moist

More fertilizer does not mean healthier plants.

Growth Slows Sometimes — That's Normal

Plants don't grow at the same pace all the time.

Growth naturally slows after planting, during temperature changes, or when plants are adjusting to new conditions. That doesn't mean they're hungry. Feeding too soon or too often can actually create more problems than it solves.

Before adding fertilizer, pause and observe. If the plant looks stable and healthy, give it time. Growth will pick back up when conditions are right.

Liquid vs Slow-Release Fertilizers

You don't need a shelf full of products.

Liquid Fertilizers

- fast-acting
- easy to dilute
- good for quick support
- must be used carefully

Slow-Release Fertilizers

- feed gradually
- lower risk of overfeeding
- convenient for busy gardeners

Both can work. Choose what fits your comfort level.

How Often Should You Feed?

There is no one-size answer.

General guideline:

- start light and infrequent
- feed less often than the label suggests
- observe how plants respond

When in doubt, use less.

Feeding New vs Established Plants

Newly planted:

- do not need immediate feeding
- focus on root establishment first

Established plants:

- benefit more from gentle feeding
- especially when flowering or fruiting

Let plants settle before adding nutrients. For general container feeding rhythms you can adjust based on observation, you'll find a Feeding Rhythm Chart in the Resources section at the back of this book.

Water First, Feed Second

Never feed dry soil.

Always:

- water first
- then feed diluted fertilizer
- this protects roots and prevents burn

Organic vs Synthetic Fertilizers

You don't need to choose sides.

Organic options:

- work more slowly
- improve soil over time

Synthetic options:

- act quickly
- easy to control

Both can be used responsibly. Choose what aligns with your comfort and access.

Common Feeding Mistakes to Avoid

Let's keep you out of trouble:

- feeding too early
- feeding too often
- using full-strength fertilizer
- feeding stressed plants
- thinking fertilizer fixes poor light or watering

Fertilizer supports good care — it doesn't replace it.

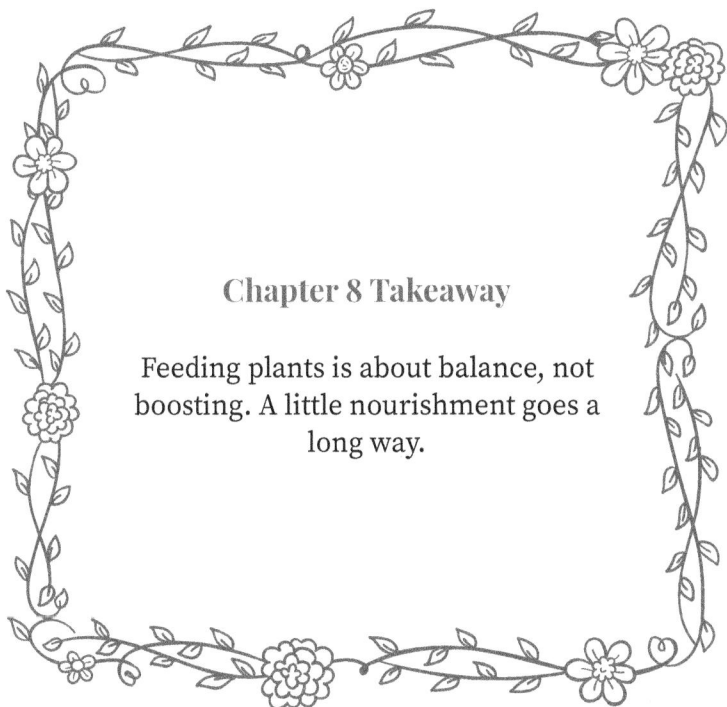

Chapter 8 Takeaway

Feeding plants is about balance, not boosting. A little nourishment goes a long way.

CHAPTER 09

Growing Methods You Might See Online

Growing Methods You Might See Online

If you've spent any time online looking up plants, you've probably seen setups that make growing look sleek, fast, and almost effortless.

Tower gardens. Countertop machines. Wall planters. DIY hacks with bottles and jars. It can start to feel like everyone else knows something you don't.

Sis, you're not behind. You're just seeing highlights, not the whole picture. Don't let social media fool you!

This chapter isn't here to tell you what you *should* use. It's here to help you understand what you're seeing so you can decide what actually fits your space, time, and comfort level.

Why Online Growing Looks So Easy

Most online content shows:

- carefully staged setups
- perfect lighting
- frequent maintenance (that you don't see)
- edited results

What you *don't* see:

- the learning curve
- the daily upkeep
- the trial and error
- the cost over time

Growing didn't suddenly get easier — it just got more shareable. If you want to compare common growing methods side by side, you'll find a Growing Method Comparison Guide in the Resources section at the back of this book — but don't worry, we'll walk through the details right here too.

Countertop Hydroponic Machines

These are some of the most popular growing tools you'll see online.

What they are

Plug-in systems that grow plants in water instead of soil, usually with built-in lights and pumps.

What they grow well

- herbs
- lettuce
- greens
- small plants

Pros

- clean and compact
- fast growth
- built-in lighting
- works without outdoor space

Cons

- higher upfront cost
- requires electricity
- regular maintenance
- limited plant size
- not "set it and forget it"

Who they're best for

- people who enjoy tech
- those with limited natural light
- folks who like structured systems

Who should skip them (for now)

- anyone overwhelmed by gadgets
- those who don't want daily monitoring
- people who prefer soil-based growing

A hydroponic machine is an option — not a shortcut.

Vertical Growing Systems

Vertical gardens save space by growing upward instead of outward.

Why they look appealing

- small footprint
- high plant count
- visually impressive

What makes them tricky

- uneven watering
- light challenges
- weight and stability issues
- more frequent maintenance

Vertical systems work best outdoors with strong light and regular attention. Indoors, they often require more effort than expected.

Self-Watering Containers

These containers include a water reservoir meant to supply moisture over time.

When they help

- consistent moisture
- busy schedules
- larger containers

Common misunderstandings

- they don't eliminate observation
- they don't fix drainage issues
- they don't work for every plant

Self-watering means *assisted* watering — not automatic success.

Grow Bags and Fabric Pots

Grow bags are popular for patios and outdoor growing.

Pros

- lightweight
- breathable
- affordable

Cons

- dry out quickly
- require frequent watering
- less forgiving in hot weather

They work well outdoors but can be challenging indoors or for beginners.

DIY Hacks and Viral Tips

Social media is full of creative ideas:

- soda bottle planters
- eggshell fertilizer
- coffee grounds everywhere
- ice cubes for watering
- rocks at the bottom of pots

Some of these ideas:

- work temporarily
- need more context
- oversimplify complex needs

Before trying a hack, ask:

- does this fit what I already know about water, light, and soil?
- is this solving a real problem — or just looking clever?

How to Decide What's Worth Trying

Instead of asking:

"Why can't I grow like that?"

Ask:

- does this fit my space?
- does this fit my schedule?
- does this fit my comfort level?
- does this support what I've already learned?

If it adds stress, complexity, or pressure — it's probably not the right fit *right now*.

If you want help deciding whether a growing method fits your lifestyle, you'll find an "Is This Growing Method Right for Me?" Checklist in the Resources section at the back of this book.

You Don't Need Every Method

Let me tell you something important.

You don't need:

- fancy systems
- trendy tools
- expensive setups

You need:

- light
- water
- patience
- observation

Everything else is optional.

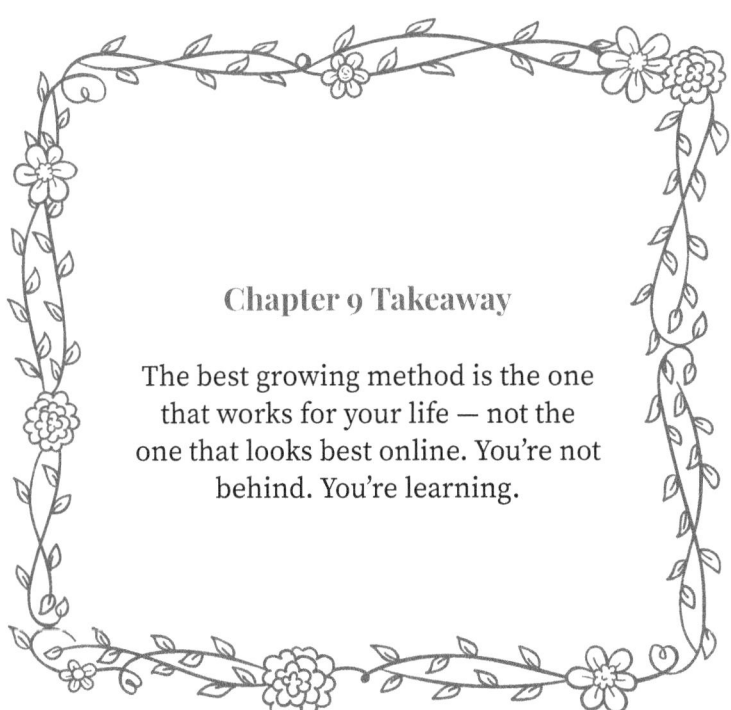

Chapter 9 Takeaway

The best growing method is the one that works for your life — not the one that looks best online. You're not behind. You're learning.

CHAPTER 10

Flowers, Fruit, and Productivity

Flowers, Fruit, and Productivity

Let's talk about expectations. A lot of people start gardening because they picture:

- flowers everywhere
- bowls of vegetables
- plants producing nonstop

And then… the plant grows leaves. Maybe flowers. But no fruit. Or one tomato. Or nothing at all.

Listen, productivity in containers looks different than what we imagine, and that doesn't mean you're doing it wrong.

This chapter will help you understand what productivity really means, why flowers don't always turn into fruit, and how to support your plants *without frustration, panic, or forcing results.*

What Productivity Looks Like in Containers

In container gardening, productivity is about health first, not volume. A productive plant may:

- grow steadily
- hold strong leaves
- produce some flowers
- yield a few fruits over time

That counts.

Containers naturally limit:

- root space
- nutrient access
- water reserves

So productivity becomes about progress, not abundance. Container gardening rewards patience more than pressure.

Flowers vs Fruit: What's the Difference?

Here's something many people don't realize at first:

Flowers and fruit are not the same thing.

- flowers are preparation
- fruit happens only *after* successful pollination

A plant can flower beautifully and still never produce fruit — especially in containers.

That's not failure. That's biology.

Why Flowers Don't Always Turn Into Fruit

There are several common reasons flowers don't become fruit:

- lack of pollination
- heat or temperature stress
- inconsistent watering
- too much nitrogen
- limited root space

Sometimes it's just one of these. Sometimes it's a combination. And sometimes the plant is simply protecting itself.

Pollination Basics for Patios and Indoors

Outdoors, pollinators like bees and wind do most of the work.

On patios and indoors, pollination often needs help.

Self-pollinating vs cross-pollinating plants

- self-pollinating plants (like tomatoes and peppers) can pollinate themselves, but still benefit from movement and airflow.
- cross-pollinating plants (like squash and cucumbers) need pollen moved from male flowers to female flowers.

Balconies, patios, and indoor spaces reduce airflow and pollinator access — so flowers may open, but pollen doesn't always move.

Ways to support pollination:

- place plants outdoors when possible
- encourage airflow
- gently shake flowering plants *(this helps pollen move when bees and breezes aren't around)*
- use a soft brush or cotton swab to transfer pollen

You're not forcing fruit — you're helping the process along.

For a simple overview of pollination support in small spaces, you'll find a Pollination Help Guide in the Resources section at the back of this book.

Big Sis Reminder

Flowers are a sign of potential, not a promise.

Flower Drop: When Blooms Fall Off

One of the most frustrating moments is seeing flowers form... then fall.

This is called flower drop, and it's common.

Common causes include:

- heat stress
- sudden temperature changes
- inconsistent watering
- excess nitrogen
- stress from moving the plant

Flower drop is often the plant conserving energy. It doesn't mean the plant is done — it means conditions weren't right *at that moment*. If you want help deciding when flower drop is normal and when adjustments may help, see the Flower Drop Guide in the Resources section.

Leaf Growth vs Flowering Growth

Plants are always balancing energy.

- leaf growth supports survival
- flowers and fruit require extra energy

When conditions are stressful, plants prioritize leaves over fruit — and that's smart.

Too much nitrogen encourages lush leaves but can delay flowering and fruiting, especially in containers where nutrients build up quickly.

If your plant is leafy but not flowering, it may be well-fed — just not ready. If you're not sure whether your plant is focused on leaves or fruit right now, the Leaf vs Fruit Growth Quick Reference in the Resources section can help.

Container Size and Root Limits

Root space directly affects productivity.

When roots feel crowded:

- flowering may slow
- fruit size may shrink
- production may pause

Signs a container may be limiting productivity:

- frequent wilting
- slowed growth despite good care
- reduced flowering over time

Sometimes upsizing helps. Sometimes the plant has simply reached its natural limit for that container.

Either way — it's not a personal failure.

Temperature, Stress, and Timing

Patio and balcony plants experience:

- heat reflected from walls
- strong wind
- sudden temperature swings

High heat often causes:

- flower drop
- reduced pollination
- temporary pauses in production

Plants may stop producing during stressful periods and resume later when conditions improve.

Waiting is often the right response.

Why One Tomato Is Still a Win

Let's reset expectations.

If you:

- grew a plant
- kept it alive
- learned how it behaves
- harvested even one thing

You succeeded.

Container gardening is cumulative. Each season builds skill, awareness, and confidence.

Supporting Productivity (Without Forcing It)

What actually helps:

- consistent watering
- adequate light
- gentle, appropriate feeding
- enough container space
- patience

What doesn't help:

- overfeeding
- constant adjusting
- panic pruning
- comparing to social media

Plants respond best to steady care — not urgency.

Harvesting Encourages Growth

When appropriate:

- harvest regularly
- pick ripe produce
- remove spent flowers

This signals the plant to continue producing *when conditions allow.*

When Productivity Slows or Stops

Sometimes plants:

- take breaks
- pause during extreme weather
- slow near the end of their life cycle

Not every pause needs fixing.

Some seasons are about learning, not harvesting.

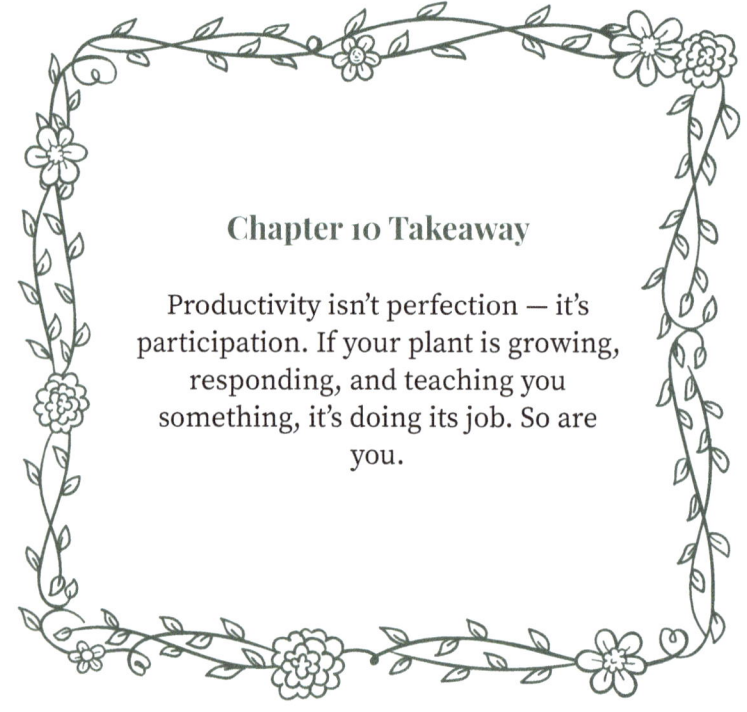

Chapter 10 Takeaway

Productivity isn't perfection — it's participation. If your plant is growing, responding, and teaching you something, it's doing its job. So are you.

CHAPTER 11

Pests & Problems Without Panic

Pests & Problems Without Panic

Let's get this out of the way right now. If you grow plants, something will show up. A bug. A spot. A chewed leaf. A surprise visitor you didn't invite.

Sis, listen — this does *not* mean you're doing something wrong. It means you're gardening.

This chapter will help you respond calmly, protect your plants thoughtfully, and decide when to act and when to let things be.

Why Pests and Problems Happen

Plants attract life.

When you grow plants on patios, balconies, or indoors, you create:

- shelter
- food
- moisture

That naturally draws insects, birds, and sometimes curious animals. Most issues happen because:

- plants are stressed
- conditions shifted
- nature noticed your setup

Not because you failed.

First Rule: Pause Before You Act

Your first instinct might be to:

- spray something
- move everything
- panic-Google symptoms

Pause.

Most problems look worse than they are, especially early on.

Before doing anything:

- look closely
- check soil moisture
- observe patterns over a few days

Many issues resolve on their own with time.

Common Pests You Might See

You don't need to memorize bugs — just recognize patterns.

Indoors

- fungus gnats
- aphids
- spider mites

Often linked to:

- overwatering
- poor airflow
- dry indoor air

Patios & Balconies

- aphids
- caterpillars
- beetles
- birds pecking seedlings
- squirrels digging in containers

Outdoor plants will always experience *some* interaction with wildlife.

That's normal.

For a quick way to tell when pests need attention and when observation is enough, see the Common Pests: Observe Before You React guide in the Resources section.

Protecting Your Plants (Without Turning Your Space into a Fortress)

Protection is about discouraging, not controlling nature.

Outdoor Patios & Balconies

Common challenges:

- birds pulling seedlings
- squirrels digging
- wind knocking plants over

Helpful strategies:

- place containers close to walls or corners
- use lightweight netting when seedlings are young
- cover soil surfaces to discourage digging
- use heavier pots or weights for stability

Some loss is part of the process. Protect what you can — release the rest.

Indoor Growing Protection

Indoor threats look different.

What to watch for:

- curious pets
- kids touching or pulling leaves
- drafts from vents or windows
- very dry air

Simple adjustments:

- place plants out of reach
- rotate away from vents
- increase airflow gently
- be mindful of sudden temperature shifts

Protection indoors is often about environment, not pests.

For simple ways to protect plants in small spaces without overdoing it, you'll find a Plant Protection Basics guide in the Resources section.

When to Intervene — and When to Let It Go

Not every issue needs fixing.

You may want to intervene when:

- damage spreads quickly
- new growth is affected
- the plant looks stressed overall

You can often wait when:

- damage is minor or cosmetic
- only a few leaves are affected
- the plant continues growing

Intervening too quickly can cause more harm than waiting.

Gentle Responses Before Big Ones

Start small.

Before reaching for sprays:

- rinse pests off with water
- remove damaged leaves
- improve airflow
- adjust watering habits

Strong treatments should be a last resort — not a first response.

Big Sis Reminder

A chewed leaf means something found your plant — not that you failed.

Recurring Problems Are Information

If the same issue keeps returning, it's a signal.

Ask:

- is watering consistent?
- is airflow adequate?
- is the plant stressed?
- is this seasonal?

Problems repeating doesn't mean you're bad at this — it means something needs adjusting.

When to Call It a Learning Season

Sometimes the most productive thing you can do is learn.

If a plant struggles despite your care:

- you gained experience
- you learned what didn't work
- you built confidence

That season still counts.

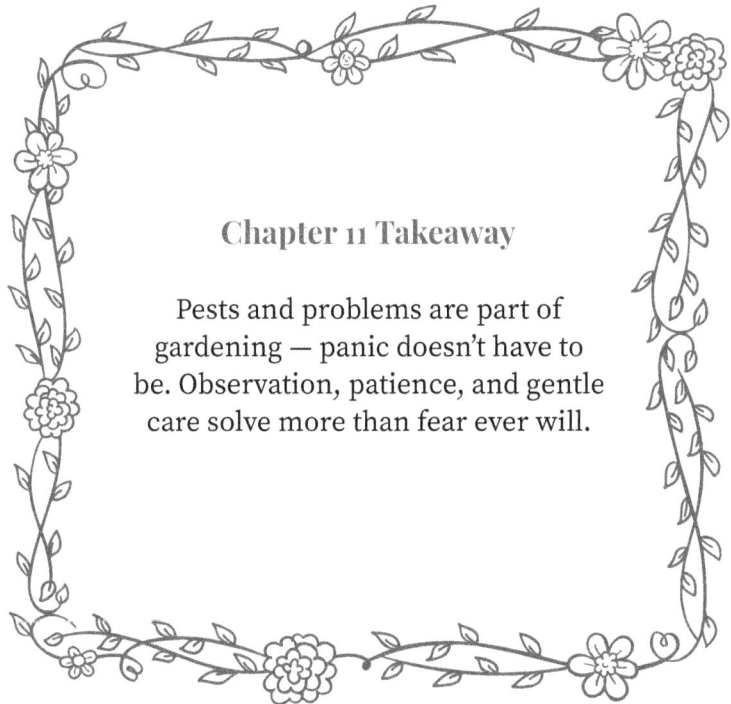

Chapter 11 Takeaway

Pests and problems are part of gardening — panic doesn't have to be. Observation, patience, and gentle care solve more than fear ever will.

CHAPTER 12

Seasonal Care & Long-Term Success

Seasonal Care & Long-Term Success

One of the quiet truths about gardening is this: what works right now won't always work later. Light shifts throughout the year. Temperatures rise and fall. Days grow longer, then shorter. As those changes happen, plants naturally speed up or slow down their growth — even when they're grown in containers, on patios, or indoors.

Sis, listen — if you've been doing your routine and what was working before isn't working now, you didn't suddenly mess up. Something shifted.

This chapter will help you understand how seasonal shifts affect container-grown plants and how long-term success comes from adjusting with awareness, not pushing harder.

Seasons Still Matter — Even Indoors

Even if you grow plants:

- in an apartment
- on a covered balcony
- near a sunny window

They still respond to:

- day length
- temperature changes
- light intensity
- humidity shifts

You may not feel the season changing indoors — but your plants do. Growth slows, water needs change, and energy shifts whether we notice or not.

What Seasonal Changes Look Like in Containers

As seasons change, you may notice:

- slower growth
- fewer flowers or fruit
- smaller or softer leaves
- soil staying wet longer or drying faster

These changes are signals, not problems. Plants are adjusting their pace to match their environment.

For a general sense of how care often shifts with the seasons for many container plants, you'll find the Seasonal Care Adjustments at a Glance guide in the Resources section at the back of this book.

Watering Changes with the Seasons

Seasonal shifts affect watering more than almost anything else.

In warmer, brighter months:

- plants use water faster
- soil dries more quickly
- containers may need frequent checks

In cooler or darker months:

- growth slows
- soil holds moisture longer
- overwatering becomes more common

One of the most helpful seasonal adjustments is simply watering less often when growth slows.

Feeding Less Is Often the Right Move

When plants slow down, feeding should slow down too.

During active growth:

- light feeding can support flowers and fruit

During slower seasons:

- extra fertilizer often does more harm than good
- plants may not use added nutrients
- salt buildup becomes more likely

Long-term success often comes from knowing when to pause feeding, not increase it.

Light Shifts Throughout the Year

Light changes even when plants don't move.

You may notice:

- shorter days
- weaker sunlight
- sun shifting away from windows
- shadows lasting longer

When light decreases:

- growth slows
- flowering may pause
- plants conserve energy

Sometimes the best adjustment is acceptance, not rearranging your whole space.

Temperature Stress Is Seasonal Too

Patios and balconies experience:

- sudden heat waves
- cold snaps
- wind exposure

Indoors, stress can come from:

- heating systems
- air conditioning
- dry winter air

Seasonal stress can cause:

- leaf drop
- paused growth
- temporary decline

This doesn't mean the plant is dying — it means it's responding.

Long-Term Success Is About Patterns, Not Perfection

Plants don't need perfect care every day.

They need:

- consistency over time
- observation
- gentle adjustments
- room to rest

Long-term success looks like:

- learning how your space behaves
- recognizing seasonal rhythms
- adjusting expectations as conditions change

This is how confidence grows.

When to Scale Back — and When to Lean In

There will be seasons when:

- you do less
- you observe more
- you let plants rest

And seasons when:

- growth picks up
- care increases naturally
- productivity returns

Both are part of the same cycle. If you're unsure whether a seasonal change needs action or patience, see the When to Adjust vs When to Leave Plants Alone Guide in the Resources section.

Gardening Is a Long Game

The most successful gardeners aren't the ones who do the most.

They're the ones who:

- stay curious
- learn from slow periods
- don't quit after one hard season

Every year adds experience — even the quiet ones.

Big Sis Reminder

You don't force plants to grow the same way all year. You just have to notice when things change and adjust your care.

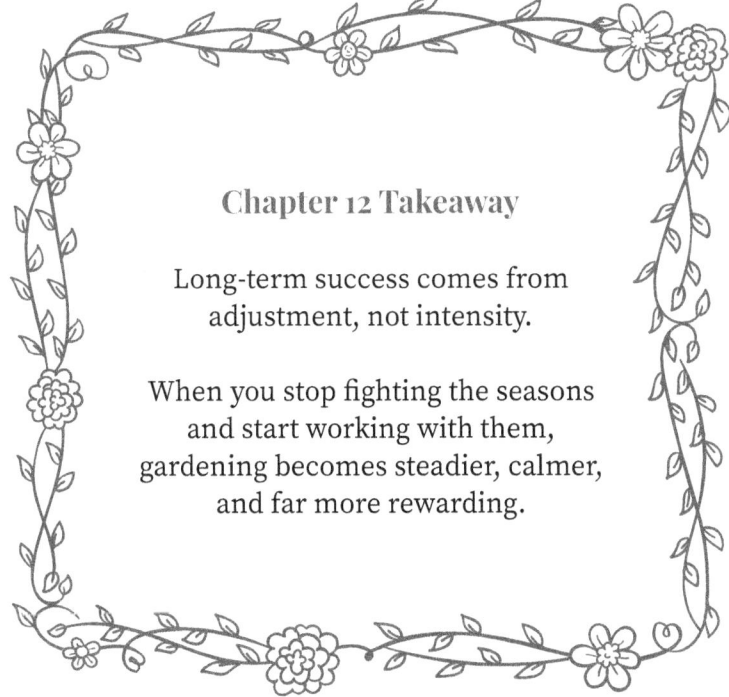

Chapter 12 Takeaway

Long-term success comes from adjustment, not intensity.

When you stop fighting the seasons and start working with them, gardening becomes steadier, calmer, and far more rewarding.

CHAPTER

13

Making Gardening Fit Your Life

Making Gardening Fit Your Life

Let's be honest for a moment. A lot of people quit gardening not because they can't grow plants — but because they feel like they're failing at some imaginary standard they never agreed to.

Let me tell you something — gardening is not supposed to stress you out.

This chapter is about shaping gardening to fit *your* life, your schedule, your energy, and your space — not forcing yourself to fit someone else's version of what a "good gardener" looks like.

There Is No One Right Way to Garden

Some people garden every day.
Some people check plants once a week.
Some grow five things.
Some grow one.

All of those count.

Gardening success is not measured by:

- how early you wake up
- how many plants you own
- how perfect everything looks

It's measured by whether gardening adds something positive to your life.

Start With the Life You Actually Have

Before choosing plants or systems, ask yourself:

- how much time do I realistically have?
- am I home often or gone a lot?
- do I want daily interaction or low maintenance?
- do I enjoy tending — or just watching things grow?

There is no "right" answer here — only honest ones.

When gardening fits your life, consistency becomes easier.

Designing for Your Energy Level

Your energy matters just as much as sunlight.

Some seasons of life support:

- frequent watering
- regular harvesting
- hands-on care

Other seasons call for:

- fewer plants
- hardy varieties
- slower rhythms

Choosing plants that match your current capacity is wisdom — not giving up.

It's Okay to Grow Less

Growing fewer plants often leads to:

- better care
- less stress
- more enjoyment
- higher success

More plants don't equal more joy.

One well-tended plant can be more satisfying than ten stressed ones.

Build Gardening Into Existing Routines

Gardening doesn't have to be a separate task.

Try pairing it with:

- morning coffee
- evening wind-down
- checking the mail
- letting the dog out

Small, consistent moments add up — and they're easier to keep.

Give Yourself Permission to Pause

There will be weeks when:

- plants don't get pruned
- logs don't get filled out
- routines loosen

That's okay. Gardening isn't a test. It's a relationship. You're allowed to pause without quitting.

Learning Seasons Still Count

Not every season will be abundant.

Some seasons are for:

- observation
- learning
- adjusting
- resting

Those seasons are just as valuable as harvest seasons. Experience builds quietly.

Let Gardening Support Your Life — Not Compete With It

Gardening should:

- ground you
- teach patience
- bring calm
- offer small wins

If it starts to feel heavy, that's a sign to adjust — not abandon it.

Big Sis Reminder

Gardening should meet you where you are — not demand you become someone else.

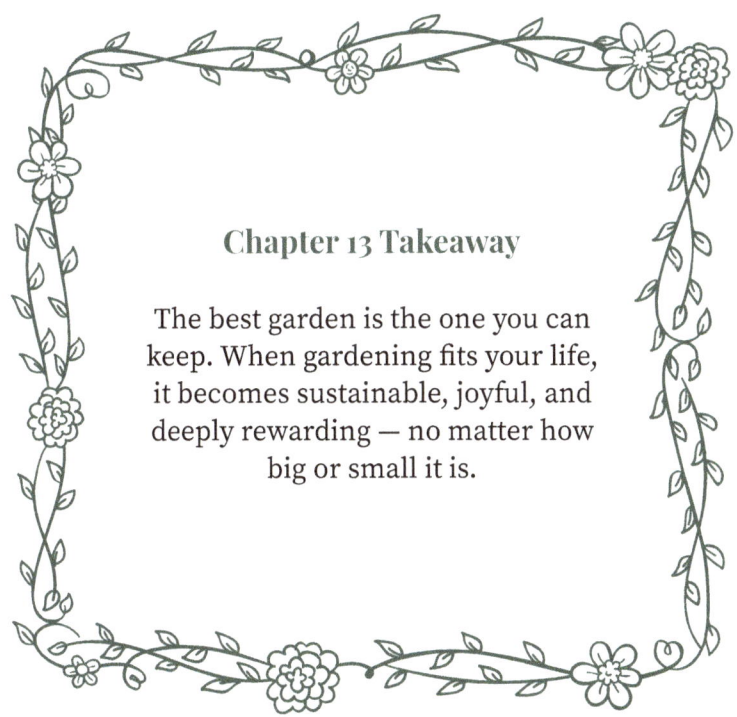

Chapter 13 Takeaway

The best garden is the one you can keep. When gardening fits your life, it becomes sustainable, joyful, and deeply rewarding — no matter how big or small it is.

CHAPTER 14

Growing Confidence, Not Just Plants

Growing Confidence, Not Just Plants

If there's one thing I hope you carry with you after reading this book, it's this: you can garden and do it confidently. When I started gardening, I honestly thought everyone else had some kind of secret. Like there was a gardening gene I missed, or a rulebook everybody else read but me. I stood over soil second-guessing everything — how deep, how often, is this even the right plant?

Every confident gardener you admire once stood exactly where you are now. I know I did.

Confidence doesn't come before the planting. It comes *from* it.

Confidence Grows the Same Way Plants Do

Confidence doesn't show up loud and fully formed. It grows the same way plants do — slowly, unevenly, and sometimes awkwardly.

It grows through:

- showing up
- paying attention
- messing up
- trying again

When I started, I killed plants. Repeatedly. I used to joke that I had a black thumb, but honestly, I was just learning — and learning takes time.

Every time you notice something new, even when it's a mistake, that's growth. Especially when you don't quit.

You Learned More Than You Realize

Even if:

- a plant didn't make it
- something didn't grow the way you pictured
- you had to start over

You still learned.

I didn't always realize it in the moment, but each season taught me something — about light, about water, about patience. Gardening has a way of slowing you down whether you want it to or not. Those lessons stay with you longer than any single harvest.

Small Gardens Still Matter

A countertop garden matters.
A balcony container matters.
One plant by a window matters.

When I started, I thought "real" gardening had to be big. Big beds, big yields, big everything. It took me a while to understand that small spaces don't make the learning smaller — they actually make it clearer. Small gardens ask you to pay attention. And attention builds confidence.

Gardening Is a Relationship, Not a Performance

Some seasons feel easy.
Some seasons feel like work.
Some seasons are quiet.

I've had all of them — sometimes back-to-back. There were times my plants thrived and times they barely made it, and both taught me something. Gardening isn't about showing off. It's about showing up.

You're Allowed to Keep It Simple

You don't have to grow everything.
You don't have to do what's trending.
You don't have to prove anything.

I used to think doing more meant I was doing better. Turns out, doing *what fits* is what actually lasts. Your garden is allowed to match your life — not compete with it.

If You Remember Nothing Else, Remember This

You don't need a yard.
You don't need fancy tools.
You don't need to know everything.

You just need:

- patience (even when it's hard)
- curiosity
- permission to learn as you go

That's enough. It always was.

One Last Big Sis Reminder

You didn't just grow plants — you grew confidence, patience, and trust in yourself. And that growth doesn't disappear when the season ends.

With love, honesty, and a few lessons learned the hard way,
Your Big Sis in the Garden,

-Ashley King

Resources

Resource 1: Space Assessment Worksheet

(Referenced in Chapter 1)

Understanding where your garden will live.

You don't need a lot of space to grow — you just need the right space. Use this worksheet to think through where container gardening will work best for you. Take your time. There are no right or wrong answers.

❶ Identify Your Potential Growing Spaces

List all the places where you could realistically grow a plant.

- ☐ Patio
- ☐ Balcony
- ☐ Porch
- ☐ Front stoop
- ☐ Window sill
- ☐ Kitchen counter near a window
- ☐ Other: _____

❷ Choose Your First Focus Area

You don't need to use every space. Choose one place to start.

My first growing space will be:

_____
_____
_____
_____
_____

③ Light Check

Think about the light this space receives.

- **Time of day with the most light:**
  ☐ Morning ☐ Midday ☐ Afternoon ☐ Evening ☐ Unsure

- **Approximate hours of light:**
  ☐ Less than 4 ☐ 4–6 ☐ 6+ ☐ Not sure yet

- **Is the light direct or filtered?**
  ☐ Direct ☐ Filtered ☐ Mostly shade

④ Accessibility & Comfort

Be honest — this matters long-term.

- Can I reach this space comfortably? ☐ Yes ☐ No
- Will I remember to water plants here? ☐ Yes ☐ Maybe ☐ No
- Is this space easy to check daily? ☐ Yes ☐ No
- Does this space feel safe and stable for containers? ☐ Yes ☐ No

⑤ Environmental Factors

Check any that apply.

☐ Windy
☐ Gets very hot
☐ Limited drainage
☐ Shared space
☐ Weight limits
☐ Pets or children nearby

Notes:
_____
_____
_____
_____

⑥ Lifestyle Fit

Answer honestly.

- How much time can I give this space each week?
  ☐ 5–10 minutes ☐ 15–30 minutes ☐ More

- How many plants do I realistically want to care for right now?
  ☐ 1–2 ☐ 3–5 ☐ More later

⑦ Final Decision

Based on everything above, this is a good place for me to start because:

_____
_____
_____
_____
_____
_____
_____
_____
_____
_____
_____
_____
_____
_____
_____
_____
_____
_____
_____
_____

Resource 2: Light Observation Worksheet

(Referenced in Chapter 2)

Understanding how light moves through your space.

Light is the most important factor in container and indoor gardening. This worksheet will help you notice patterns over time so you can choose plants that actually thrive where you live. You don't need exact measurements — just honest observation.

❶ Identify the Space

Where are you observing light?

☐ Kitchen window
☐ Living room window
☐ Bedroom window
☐ Patio / porch
☐ Balcony
☐ Other: _____

❷ Window or Location Details

(If applicable)

- Approximate window direction (if known):
  ☐ North ☐ South ☐ East ☐ West ☐ Not sure

- Is the light mostly:
  ☐ Direct (sun hits the space)
  ☐ Bright but indirect
  ☐ Mostly shade

③ Observe the Light Over a Day

Check in at different times. You can do this in one day or spread it over several days.

Time of Day	Is there direct sun?	Bright light?	Shade?
Morning	☐ Yes ☐ No	☐ Yes ☐ No	☐ Yes ☐ No
Midday	☐ Yes ☐ No	☐ Yes ☐ No	☐ Yes ☐ No
Afternoon	☐ Yes ☐ No	☐ Yes ☐ No	☐ Yes ☐ No
Evening	☐ Yes ☐ No	☐ Yes ☐ No	☐ Yes ☐ No

④ Estimate Light Duration

Based on your observations, this space receives approximately:

☐ Less than 4 hours of direct sun
☐ 4–6 hours of direct sun
☐ 6+ hours of direct sun
☐ Unsure (still observing)

⑤ Environmental Notes

Check any that apply:

☐ Very warm in afternoon
☐ Strong glare or heat through glass
☐ Shade from buildings, trees, or railings
☐ Light changes seasonally
☐ Wind exposure (outdoors)

Notes:

_____
_____
_____
_____

6 What This Light Is Best Suited For

Based on what you've observed, this space is likely good for:

☐ Herbs
☐ Leafy greens
☐ Flowering plants
☐ Fruit-bearing plants
☐ Decorative plants
☐ Grow light support may be helpful

7 Final Takeaway

One thing I learned about this space:

_____
_____
_____
_____
_____

Big Sis Reminder

Light doesn't have to be perfect — it just needs to be understood.

Resource 3: Container Selection Worksheet

(Referenced in Chapter 3)

Choosing containers that work for your plants — and for you.

The right container makes gardening easier. Use this worksheet to choose containers that fit your space, your plants, and your daily routine.

❶ Identify Where This Container Will Live

Check one:

☐ Patio
☐ Balcony
☐ Porch
☐ Front stoop
☐ Window sill
☐ Countertop
☐ Other: _____

Indoor or outdoor? ☐ Indoor ☐ Outdoor

❷ What Will You Grow in This Container?

(Choose one primary plant type)

☐ Herbs
☐ Leafy greens
☐ Vegetables
☐ Flowers
☐ Fruit plant
☐ Mixed planting
Plant name (if known): _____

③ Size Matters

Based on what you're growing, this container should be:

☐ Small (frequent watering, limited growth)
☐ Medium (balanced, manageable)
☐ Large (more forgiving, less frequent watering)

Notes:

_____
_____
_____
_____

④ Container Material Preference

Check what fits your needs:

☐ Lightweight (plastic, resin, fabric)
☐ Breathable (terracotta, fabric)
☐ Decorative (ceramic, glazed)
☐ Durable (wood, resin)

Important to me:

☐ Easy to move
☐ Holds moisture well
☐ Dries quickly
☐ Looks good in my space

⑤ Drainage Check

This container:

☐ Has drainage holes
☐ Needs drainage holes added
☐ Will be used as a cover pot
☐ Is not suitable for planting directly

6 Accessibility & Comfort

Be honest — this matters long-term.

☐ I can lift this when it's full
☐ I can water it easily
☐ It won't tip over
☐ It's placed at a comfortable height

7 Final Decision

This container works for me because:

_____
_____
_____
_____
_____
_____
_____
_____
_____
_____
_____
_____
_____
_____
_____
_____
_____

Big Sis Reminder

A container that fits your life will always outperform one that just looks good.

Resource 4: Soil Troubleshooting Chart

(Referenced in Chapter 4)

Common container soil problems and what they usually mean.

Use this chart when something feels "off" with your soil. These issues are common in container gardening and usually easy to fix.

What You Notice	What's Likely Happening	What to Do
Water runs straight through the pot	Soil is too dry, broken down, or pulling away from the sides	Water slowly and deeply; refresh soil if needed
Water sits on top of the soil	Soil is compacted or drainage is poor	Loosen soil gently; check drainage holes; refresh mix
Soil stays wet for days	Container too large, poor drainage, or overwatering	Allow soil to dry slightly; adjust watering habits
Fungus gnats	Soil staying consistently moist	Let soil dry between waterings; improve airflow
Soil feels hard or crusty	Organic matter depleted	Mix in fresh potting mix or compost
Plants wilt but soil is wet	Roots may be stressed or suffocating	Improve drainage; avoid watering again immediately
Yellowing leaves with slow growth	Roots struggling to access oxygen or nutrients	Check soil structure; refresh or repot if needed
Soil smells sour or musty	Poor aeration or root rot risk	Remove plant, assess roots, replace soil if necessary

Big Sis Reminder

Most soil problems don't mean you failed — they mean your soil needs attention.

Resource 5: Soil Refresh Worksheet

(Referenced in Chapter 4)

Deciding when to reuse, refresh, or replace container soil.

Soil doesn't last forever — especially in containers. Use this worksheet to decide what your soil needs right now, without guessing.

❶ Identify the Container

What plant was growing here?
Plant type: _____
Container size/material: _____
Indoor or outdoor: ☐ Indoor ☐ Outdoor

❷ How Did the Plant Do?

Be honest — this helps.
☐ Grew well and stayed healthy
☐ Grew slowly but survived
☐ Struggled most of the time
☐ Showed signs of disease or pests

Notes:

_____
_____
_____
_____
_____
_____

③ Check the Soil Condition

Feel and observe the soil.
☐ Loose and crumbly
☐ Compact or hard
☐ Drains quickly
☐ Stays wet too long
☐ Has a sour or musty smell
☐ Has visible pests or mold

④ Decide What to Do Next

Based on what you observed:
☐ Reuse as-is
(Soil is loose, plant was healthy, drainage is good)
☐ Refresh soil
(Add fresh potting mix or compost to improve structure)
☐ Replace soil entirely
(Plant struggled badly, disease present, soil compacted)

⑤ If Refreshing Soil

Check what you'll add:
☐ Fresh potting mix
☐ Compost
☐ Slow-release fertilizer (optional)

Notes:
_____
_____
_____
_____
_____
_____
_____
_____
_____

6 Final Decision

This soil needs:
☐ Nothing
☐ A refresh
☐ Full replacement

Why:

_____
_____
_____
_____
_____
_____
_____

Big Sis Reminder

Refreshing soil is part of container gardening — not a sign of failure.

Resource 6: Plant Selection Guide

(Referenced in Chapter 5)

What grows well in containers — and where.

This guide helps you choose plants that match your space, light, and experience level. Use it to build confidence first, then expand as you're ready.

Best Starter Plants for Containers (Beginner-Friendly)

These plants tend to forgive small mistakes and perform well in pots.

- Basil
- Parsley
- Thyme
- Mint
- Lettuce
- Spinach
- Arugula
- Green onions
- Strawberries
- Peppers (patio or compact varieties)

Best Plants for Countertops & Indoors

These grow well with limited space and light.

- Basil
- Parsley
- Mint
- Microgreens
- Baby lettuce

- Green onions
- Small flowering plants

Notes:

- Growth is slower indoors
- Harvest regularly for best results
- One or two plants is plenty to start

Best Plants for Patios & Balconies

These benefit from outdoor light and airflow.

- Tomatoes (bush or patio varieties)
- Peppers
- Strawberries
- Leafy greens
- Herbs
- Nasturtiums (edible flowers)

Plants That Do Well Together

Good container companions share similar needs.

- Lettuce + herbs
- Mixed salad greens
- Strawberries + shallow-rooted companions
- Herb-only containers

Avoid mixing:

- Large and small growers
- Heavy feeders with light feeders
- Sun lovers with shade lovers

Plants to Skip (At Least for Now)

These often frustrate beginners in containers.

- Corn
- Pumpkins
- Watermelon
- Large tomato varieties
- Broccoli
- Cauliflower
- Deep root crops in shallow pots

These plants need more:

- Space
- Feeding
- Consistency
- Patience

You can grow them — just not first.

How to Choose What to Grow First

Ask yourself:

- How much light does my space get?
- How much time do I want to spend caring for plants?
- Do I want quick harvests or long-term growth?
- Am I growing indoors or outdoors?

Start with one to three plants. Add more later.

Big Sis Reminder

The best plant is the one that fits your space and your life.

Resource 7: Plant Spacing Guide

(Referenced in Chapter 5)

How much room common container plants actually need?

Spacing matters in container gardening. Too many plants in one pot leads to competition, stress, and smaller harvests. This guide helps you choose comfort overcrowding.

One Plant Per Container (Best Solo Performers)

These plants do best when grown alone.

Plant	Recommended Container	Notes
Tomatoes (bush/patio)	5+ gallons	One plant only
Peppers	3–5 gallons	One plant per pot
Rosemary	Medium–large pot	Needs airflow
Eggplant	Large container	Heavy feeder

Multiple Plants Per Container (Group-Friendly)

Plant	Spacing	Container Tip
Lettuce	4–6 inches	Wide containers work best
Spinach	3–4 inches	Harvest outer leaves
Arugula	3–4 inches	Cut-and-come-again
Green onions	2–3 inches	Great for shallow pots

Herbs That Grow Well Together

Herbs with similar needs can share space.

Herb	Spacing	Notes
Basil	6–8 inches	Likes room to branch
Parsley	6 inches	Grows upright
Cilantro	4–6 inches	Short-lived
Thyme	6–8 inches	Low-growing

Avoid mixing:

Mint with other herbs (it spreads fast)

Special Cases

Plant	Spacing Notes
Strawberries	8–10 inches
Microgreens	Dense sowing
Flowers	Follow seed packet

Signs a Container Is Overcrowded

- Plants stay small
- Leaves overlap heavily
- Soil dries out very quickly
- Poor airflow
- Fewer harvests

When in doubt: remove one plant. It usually helps the others.

Big Sis Reminder

More plants don't mean more food. More space often does.

Resource 8: Planting Depth Guide

(Referenced in Chapter 6)

How deep to plant common container plants?

Planting depth affects root health, stability, and growth. Most container plants do best when planted at the same depth they were growing before — with a few important exceptions. Use this guide as a quick check before planting.

Plant at the Same Depth (Most Plants)

These plants should be planted so the top of the soil matches the original soil line.

- Herbs (basil, parsley, thyme, cilantro, mint*)
- Lettuce and leafy greens
- Peppers
- Strawberries
- Flowers
- Green onions

*Mint spreads aggressively — give it space, not depth.

Tomatoes: Plant Deeper Than the Original Soil Line

Tomatoes benefit from being planted deeper than they were in their original container.

- Bury part of the stem
- Roots will form along the buried stem
- Results in stronger plants

Remove lower leaves before planting deeper.

Shallow Rooted Plants

These plants prefer shallower planting and wide containers.

- Lettuce
- Spinach
- Microgreens
- Strawberries

Do not bury stems deeply — roots sit closer to the surface.

Avoid Planting Too Deep

Planting too deep can cause:

- Stem rot
- Slow growth
- Yellowing leaves

If the stem disappears under soil, it's probably too deep.

Avoid Planting Too Shallow

Planting too shallow can cause:

- Roots drying out
- Unstable plants
- Wilting

Roots should be fully covered and supported.

Quick Rule of Thumb

Match the soil line you see — unless you're planting tomatoes.

Big Sis Reminder

Planting depth doesn't need to be exact — it just needs to be thoughtful.

Resource 9: Planting Day Checklist

(Referenced in Chapter 6)

A simple guide to help you plant with confidence.

Use this checklist before and during planting to slow down, stay focused, and avoid common mistakes. You don't need to rush — plants appreciate intention.

Before You Start

- ☐ Chosen the right plant for my space
- ☐ Selected a container with drainage holes
- ☐ Checked container size and stability
- ☐ Gathered potting mix
- ☐ Have water nearby
- ☐ Read the planting depth guidance

Preparing the Container

- ☐ Container is clean
- ☐ Drainage holes are open
- ☐ Soil added about two-thirds full
- ☐ Soil is loose, not packed

Planting

- ☐ Plant removed gently from nursery pot
- ☐ Roots loosened if tightly bound
- ☐ Planted at correct depth
- ☐ Soil filled in around plant
- ☐ About 1 inch of space left at top

After Planting

☐ Watered slowly and thoroughly
☐ Excess water drained out
☐ Container placed in its intended spot
☐ Plant left alone to settle in

Next 24–48 Hours

☐ Checked soil moisture (not overwatered)
☐ Expected some drooping — didn't panic
☐ Avoided moving or disturbing the plant

Big Sis Reminder

Planting doesn't have to be perfect — it just needs care and patience.

Resource 10: Watering Rhythm Guide

(Referenced in Chapter 7)

A flexible approach to watering container plants.

Watering rhythm is about patterns, not dates. This guide helps you understand when plants usually need water — while still encouraging you to check the soil first. Use this as a starting point, not a rule.

Environment	Typical Rhythm	Notes
Indoor containers	Every 5–10 days	Check soil before watering
Outdoor containers (mild weather)	Every 2–5 days	Wind increases drying
Outdoor containers (hot weather)	Daily checks	Some may need daily water
Newly planted containers	More frequent	Keep soil evenly moist
Established plants	Less frequent	Allow slight drying

Factors That Change Watering Rhythm

Your plants may need water more often if:

- Containers are small
- Weather is hot or windy
- Plants are actively growing
- Containers are in full sun

Your plants may need water less often if:

- Containers are large
- Weather is cool or cloudy
- Plants are indoors
- Soil stays moist below the surface

Container Size	Drying Speed
Small pots	Dry quickly
Medium pots	Moderate
Large pots	Hold moisture longer

Bigger containers forgive missed watering days more easily.

Plant Type Considerations

- Leafy greens prefer consistent moisture
- Herbs tolerate slight drying
- Fruiting plants need steady water
- Shallow-rooted plants dry faster

Use Rhythm + Observation Together

Always pair rhythm with:

- The finger test
- Plant appearance
- Weight of the container

If rhythm says "water" but soil feels moist — wait.

Big Sis Reminder

Consistency matters more than frequency. Observation matters more than schedules.

Resource 11: Watering Log Worksheet

(Referenced in Chapter 7)

Track patterns without overthinking.

This worksheet helps you notice how often your plants actually need water based on their environment — not guesswork. You don't need to fill this out forever. Use it for a week or two until patterns become clear.

Plant Information

- Plant name(s): _____
- Location (indoor / outdoor): _____
- Container size: _____
- Light exposure: _____

Watering Log

Date	Soil Check (Dry / Moist)	Watered? (Y/N)	Notes (weather, drooping, growth)
	☐ Dry ☐ Moist	☐ Yes ☐ No	
	☐ Dry ☐ Moist	☐ Yes ☐ No	
	☐ Dry ☐ Moist	☐ Yes ☐ No	
	☐ Dry ☐ Moist	☐ Yes ☐ No	
	☐ Dry ☐ Moist	☐ Yes ☐ No	
	☐ Dry ☐ Moist	☐ Yes ☐ No	
	☐ Dry ☐ Moist	☐ Yes ☐ No	

Weekly Observations

How often did this plant need water?

_____

Did weather or location affect watering?

_____

Did the plant look healthier, stressed, or unchanged?

_____

Big Sis Reminder

The goal isn't perfection — it's awareness. Once you see the rhythm, you can stop tracking and trust what you've learned.

Need more space? Use this extra log to continue tracking.

Date	Soil Check (Dry / Moist)	Watered? (Y/N)	Notes (weather, drooping, growth)
	☐ Dry ☐ Moist	☐ Yes ☐ No	
	☐ Dry ☐ Moist	☐ Yes ☐ No	
	☐ Dry ☐ Moist	☐ Yes ☐ No	
	☐ Dry ☐ Moist	☐ Yes ☐ No	
	☐ Dry ☐ Moist	☐ Yes ☐ No	
	☐ Dry ☐ Moist	☐ Yes ☐ No	
	☐ Dry ☐ Moist	☐ Yes ☐ No	
	☐ Dry ☐ Moist	☐ Yes ☐ No	
	☐ Dry ☐ Moist	☐ Yes ☐ No	

Resource 12: Feeding Basics Guide

(Referenced in Chapter 8)

A simple approach to nourishing container plants.

This guide covers the basics of feeding container plants without hype, pressure, or overdoing it. When in doubt, less is more.

Do All Plants Need Fertilizer?

No. Fresh potting mix already contains nutrients. Many plants grow well for weeks or months without additional feeding.

When Feeding Helps

Feeding may be helpful when:

- Plants have been growing for several weeks
- Growth has slowed
- Leaves look pale (not from overwatering)
- Plants are flowering or producing fruit
- Containers are watered frequently

When NOT to Feed

Do not fertilize when:

- Plants were recently planted
- Plants are stressed or wilting
- Soil is dry
- Growth looks steady and healthy

Types of Fertilizer (At a Glance)

- Liquid fertilizers
  - Fast-acting
  - Easy to adjust

- Must be diluted
- Higher risk of overfeeding

➤ Slow-release fertilizers
- Feed gradually
- Lower maintenance
- Lower risk
- Good for beginners

How to Feed Safely

➤ Always water first
➤ Use less than the label recommends
➤ Feed lightly and observe
➤ Do not feed repeatedly without signs

How Often Is Enough?

There is no fixed schedule, just general feeding rhythms for containers- but they must be adjusted by observation. Container plants often need feeding more regularly than plants grown in the ground, but frequency depends on the plant, container size, and fertilizer type.

General guidelines:

➤ Liquid fertilizer: every 2–4 weeks
➤ Slow-release fertilizer: every 2–3 months
➤ Heavy-feeding plants (tomatoes, peppers): may need feeding more often
➤ Leafy greens and herbs: usually need less

These are starting points — not rules. Sis, listen — feeding too often causes more problems than feeding too little. So, always observe how your plant responds before feeding again.

Beginner Rule of Thumb

If you're unsure whether to feed, wait and observe.

Big Sis Reminder

Healthy plants grow steadily — not explosively.

Resource 13: Fertilizer Decision Chart

(Referenced in Chapter 8)

A simple way to decide when — and if — to feed container plants.

Use this chart to help you decide whether your plant actually needs fertilizer right now. When in doubt, wait and observe.

Start Here

Is the plant newly planted (within the last 2–3 weeks)?

☐ Yes → **Do NOT fertilize yet**
Focus on watering and root establishment.

☐ No → Go to next question.

Check the Plant's Appearance

Does the plant look generally healthy and growing?

☐ Yes → **Feeding is likely not needed right now**
Continue regular care and observation.

☐ No → Go to next question.

Look for Feeding-Related Signs

Are you seeing signs like pale leaves, slow growth, or reduced flowering — and watering/light are already appropriate?

☐ Yes → **Feeding may be helpful.**
Start with a light, diluted fertilizer.

☐ No → Feeding may not be the issue.
Recheck watering, light, and container size.

Choose a Fertilizer Type

Do you prefer simplicity and low risk?

☐ Yes → **Use a slow-release fertilizer**
Apply at the lowest recommended rate.

☐ No → Go to the next question.

Do you want more control or quick support?

☐ Yes → **Use a liquid fertilizer, diluted more than the label suggests.**

☐ No → Do not fertilize right now.
Continue observing the plant and revisit feeding later.

Before You Feed, Ask One Last Question

Is the plant stressed (overwatered, heat-stressed, recently moved, or damaged)?

☐ Yes → **Do NOT fertilize yet**
Let the plant recover first.

☐ No → Proceed gently.

Always Remember

- Water first, feed second
- Use less than recommended
- Observe before repeating

Big Sis Reminder

Fertilizer supports good care — it doesn't replace it.

Resource 14: Feeding Rhythm Chart

(Referenced in Chapter 8)

General feeding patterns for container plants.

This chart offers starting points, not strict schedules. Always adjust based on plant response, container size, and growing conditions.

Feeding Rhythms by Fertilizer Type

Fertilizer Type	Typical Rhythm	Notes
Liquid fertilizer	Every 2–4 weeks	Dilute more than label
Slow-release fertilizer	Every 2–3 months	Apply at low rate
Compost-based feeding	Monthly	Gentle support
No fertilizer	As needed	Many plants grow well without feeding

Feeding Rhythms by Plant Type

Plant Type	Feeding Needs	Notes
Leafy greens	Low–moderate	Too much causes bitterness
Herbs	Low	Overfeeding reduces flavor
Fruiting plants	Moderate	Feed during active growth
Flowering plants	Moderate	Support blooms, don't force

Container Size Matters

Container Size	Feeding Consideration
Small containers	Nutrients wash out faster
Medium containers	Moderate feeding
Large containers	Hold nutrients longer

When to Pause Feeding

Do not fertilize when:

- Plants are stressed
- Soil is dry
- Growth is steady and healthy
- Weather is extremely hot

How to Adjust the Rhythm

- Feed less often if growth is strong
- Pause if leaves burn or growth stalls
- Resume gently when conditions improve

Big Sis Reminder

Feeding supports healthy plants — it does not replace light, water, or time.

Resource 15: Growing Method Comparison Guide

(Referenced in Chapter 9)

A side-by-side look at common growing methods.

This guide helps you compare popular growing methods you may see online. Use it to decide what fits your space, time, and comfort level — not what looks best on social media.

Growing Methods at a Glance

Growing Method	Best For	Maintenance Level	Cost	Learning Curve	Notes
Soil Containers (Pots)	Most beginners	Low–Moderate	Low	Gentle	Flexible, forgiving, adaptable
Countertop Hydroponic Machines	Herbs & greens	Moderate	High	Moderate	Structured, tech-based, fast growth
Vertical Systems	Outdoor spaces	High	Moderate–High	Steep	Light & watering challenges
Self-Watering Containers	Busy schedules	Low–Moderate	Moderate	Gentle	Still require observation
Grow Bags / Fabric Pots	Outdoor patios	Moderate	Low–Moderate	Moderate	Dry out quickly in heat

Key Differences to Consider

Soil Containers

- Most flexible option
- Easy to scale up or down
- Allows trial and error
- Works indoors or outdoors

Good choice if: you want simplicity and room to learn.

Countertop Hydroponic Machines

- Soil-free growing
- Built-in lights and pumps
- Requires electricity
- Limited plant size

Good choice if: you enjoy tech and structured systems.

Vertical Growing Systems

- Space-saving design
- Can grow many plants at once
- Uneven watering is common
- Requires strong light

Good choice if: you have outdoor space and time to maintain.

Self-Watering Containers

- Built-in water reservoir
- Helps with consistency
- Not automatic
- Not ideal for all plants

Good choice if: you want assistance, not autopilot.

Grow Bags / Fabric Pots

- Lightweight and breathable
- Affordable
- Dry out faster than pots
- Best outdoors

Good choice if: you grow outside and can water often.

Questions to Ask Yourself

Before choosing a method, ask:

- Do I want flexibility or structure?
- How much time can I give weekly?
- Do I enjoy monitoring systems?
- Am I growing indoors or outdoors?
- Am I okay with trial and error?

Big Sis Reminder

You don't need the most popular method — you need the one that works for your life.

Resource 16: Is This Growing Method Right for Me? Checklist

(Referenced in Chapter 9)

A quick checklist to help you decide before you commit.

Use this checklist to decide whether a growing method fits your space, time, and energy. There are no wrong answers — this is about alignment, not pressure.

Your Space

☐ I know where this will live (countertop, patio, window, balcony)
☐ I have enough light for this method
☐ I have room for it to stay put long-term
☐ I'm okay with how it looks in my space

Your Time

☐ I can check plants regularly (daily or every few days)
☐ I'm comfortable with ongoing care
☐ I won't mind small maintenance tasks
☐ I'm okay learning as I go

Your Comfort Level

☐ I enjoy structured systems and routines
☐ I'm comfortable troubleshooting small issues
☐ I don't mind trial and error
☐ I feel okay adjusting if something doesn't work right away

Your Care Style

☐ I prefer soil-based growing
☐ I'm open to water-based growing
☐ I like flexibility
☐ I like consistency and predictability

Your Budget

☐ I'm comfortable with the upfront cost
☐ I'm okay with replacement parts or supplies
☐ I don't feel pressured to buy something expensive to succeed

Your Expectations

☐ I understand this method has limits
☐ I'm okay starting small
☐ I value learning over perfection
☐ I know this method won't replace patience

Your Results

- Mostly checked? → This method may be a good fit.
- Many unchecked? → It might not be the right choice right now.
- Unsure? → Stick with simple containers and revisit later.

Big Sis Reminder

You don't need the most popular method — you need the one that fits your life.

Resource 17:
Pollination Help Guide

(Referenced in Chapter 10)

This guide helps you understand when pollination needs support, which plants benefit from help, and how to assist gently when growing on patios, balconies, or indoors.

What Pollination Is

Pollination happens when pollen moves from one part of a flower to another, allowing fruit to form. Outdoors, wind and pollinators usually handle this. In small or enclosed spaces, plants may need help.

Self-Pollinating vs Cross-Pollinating Plants

Self-pollinating plants

These plants can pollinate themselves but still benefit from movement.

- Tomatoes
- Peppers
- Eggplant

Cross-pollinating plants

These plants need pollen moved between separate flowers.

- Squash
- Cucumbers
- Melons

If you're growing cross-pollinating plants in containers, assistance is often necessary.

Why Pollination Can Be Limited on Patios & Indoors

- Fewer pollinators
- Reduced airflow
- Enclosed spaces
- Plants grouped tightly together

Flowers may open normally, but pollen doesn't always move on its own.

Ways to Support Pollination

You only need to assist during flowering.

- **Gently shake flowering plants**
  Helps pollen move when wind or pollinators are limited.
- **Encourage airflow**
  Natural breeze or gentle air movement helps pollen transfer.
- **Use a soft brush or cotton swab**
  Lightly move pollen between flowers if needed.
- **Place plants outdoors temporarily (if possible)**
  Even short exposure can help.

You don't need to do this every day — a few times during flowering is often enough.

Signs Pollination Was Successful

- Flowers remain attached
- Small fruit begins to form behind the flower
- Flowers dry up naturally instead of falling

What NOT to Do

- Do not force flowers open
- Do not over-handle plants
- Do not fertilize to "fix" pollination
- Do not panic if early flowers fall

Big Sis Reminder

Not every flower is meant to become fruit. Supporting pollination helps — but patience still matters.

Resource 18: Flower Drop Guide: What's Normal vs What to Adjust

(Referenced in Chapter 10)

This guide helps you understand why flowers sometimes fall off, when it's part of the plant's natural process, and when gentle adjustments may help.

What Is Flower Drop?

Flower drop happens when a plant forms flowers, but they fall off before turning into fruit. It's common in container gardening — especially on patios, balconies, and in changing weather. Flower drop does not automatically mean failure.

When Flower Drop Is Normal

Flower drop is often normal when:

- The plant is young or newly established
- Temperatures are very hot or very cool
- The plant is adjusting to a new space
- The plant is conserving energy

In these cases, the plant may flower again once conditions improve.

When Flower Drop May Need Adjustment

You may want to adjust care if flower drop happens alongside:

- Extreme heat or cold
- Inconsistent watering
- Very lush leaf growth with few flowers
- Limited airflow or pollination

Small changes often help more than big ones.

Common Causes & Gentle Responses

Heat stress
→ Provide shade during extreme heat and water consistently.

Inconsistent watering
→ Aim for steady moisture, not swings between dry and soaked.

Excess nitrogen
→ Pause feeding and allow the plant to rebalance.

Limited pollination
→ Assist gently during flowering (see Pollination Help Quick Guide).

When to Wait Instead of Fix

Sometimes the best response is patience.

Wait and observe if:

- The plant looks healthy overall
- New growth continues
- Conditions recently changed

Plants often regulate themselves once stress passes.

Big Sis Reminder

Flower drop is often a pause — not the end of the story.

Resource 19: Leaf vs Fruit Growth Quick Reference

(Referenced in Chapter 10)

This guide helps you understand what your plant is prioritizing right now and what that means for your next step — if any. Plants shift focus naturally. Leaf growth and fruiting don't always happen at the same time.

When a Plant Is Focused on Leaf Growth

What you may see:

- Lots of new leaves
- Deep green color
- Strong stems
- Few or no flowers

What this usually means:

- The plant is building strength
- Roots and leaves are being established
- Conditions favor growth, not reproduction

What to do:

- Keep care consistent
- Avoid increasing fertilizer
- Make sure light is adequate
- Be patient — flowering often comes later

When a Plant Is Focused on Flowering & Fruiting

What you may see:

- Flowers forming
- Small fruit appearing
- Slower leaf growth

What this usually means:

- The plant feels stable enough to reproduce
- Energy is shifting from leaves to fruit

What to do:

- Maintain steady watering
- Support pollination if needed
- Avoid sudden changes
- Harvest when ready to encourage continued production

When Growth Feels Unbalanced

Lots of leaves, no flowers:

- May be excess nitrogen
- May be low light
- May simply be early in the plant's life

Flowers but no fruit:

- Pollination may be limited
- Heat or stress may be present
- Flower drop may be normal

Small adjustments help more than drastic changes.

Plants Can Switch Focus

Plants move back and forth between leaf growth and fruiting depending on:

- Temperature
- Light
- Water consistency
- Stress levels
- Season

A pause in fruiting doesn't mean the plant is done.

Big Sis Reminder

A leafy plant isn't failing — it's preparing.

Resource 20: Common Pests: Observe Before You React

This guide helps you decide when pests actually need attention and when a calm pause is the best response. Not every bug or bite is an emergency.

First Things First: Don't Panic

Seeing a pest doesn't mean:

- Your plant is ruined
- You failed
- You need chemicals right away

Most pest issues start small and are manageable with simple observation.

Step 1: Look Closely

Before doing anything, check:

- Are only a few leaves affected?
- Is new growth still healthy?
- Are pests isolated to one plant?
- Has this appeared suddenly or gradually?

Minor, localized issues often resolve with time and small adjustments. Common Indoor Pests

Fungus gnats

- Usually linked to consistently wet soil
- Often more annoying than harmful

Aphids

- Cluster on new growth
- Can often be rinsed off

Spider mites

- Thrive in dry indoor air
- Look for fine webbing

Indoors, pests often signal environmental imbalance, not infestation.

Common Patio & Balcony Visitors

Aphids

- Common on new growth

Caterpillars

- Visible chewing on leaves

Birds

- Peck at seedlings or soil

Squirrels

- Dig in containers

Outdoor spaces will always attract some visitors. The goal is management, not elimination.

Step 2: Decide — Observe or Act?

You can often observe if:

- Damage is light or cosmetic
- Only a few leaves are affected

- New growth looks healthy
- The issue appeared recently

You may want to act if:

- Damage is spreading quickly
- New growth is being affected
- The plant looks stressed overall
- Multiple plants are impacted

Observation is an action — it gives you information.

Step 3: Start With Gentle Responses

Before sprays or treatments, try:

- Rinsing pests off with water
- Removing heavily damaged leaves
- Improving airflow
- Adjusting watering habits

These steps solve many early pest problems without escalating stress.

What to Avoid Early On

- Over-treating minor issues
- Mixing multiple treatments at once
- Using chemicals as a first response
- Constantly moving stressed plants

Strong reactions often cause more harm than the pests themselves.

Big Sis Reminder

Seeing a pest means your plant is part of the ecosystem — not that you're failing.

Resource 21: Plant Protection Basics (Indoors & Outdoors)

(Referenced in Chapter 11)

This guide helps you protect plants grown on patios, balconies, and indoors without overreacting or turning your space into a fortress. Protection is about awareness and small adjustments — not control.

The Goal of Plant Protection

Plant protection is about:

- Reducing stress
- Discouraging disruption
- Supporting healthy growth

It is not about eliminating every risk. Some interaction with the environment is normal.

Outdoor Protection: Patios & Balconies

Common Outdoor Challenges

- Birds pecking seedlings
- Squirrels digging in containers
- Wind tipping or drying plants
- Pets brushing past pots

Simple Ways to Protect Outdoor Plants

Placement matters

- Position containers near walls or corners
- Elevate plants off the ground when possible
- Group plants together to reduce exposure

Discourage digging

- Cover soil with mulch or decorative stones (on top, not mixed in)
- Use plant collars or lightweight mesh for seedlings

Stabilize containers

- Choose heavier pots for windy areas
- Add weight to the bottom of tall containers
- Secure lightweight containers during storms

Use netting thoughtfully

- Use lightweight netting only when needed
- Remove once plants are established
- Avoid trapping beneficial insects

Indoor Plant Protection

Indoor plants face different challenges.

Common Indoor Risks

- Curious pets
- Children pulling leaves
- Dry indoor air
- Drafts from vents or windows
- Sudden temperature changes

Simple Indoor Protection Tips

Placement

- Keep plants out of reach of pets and children
- Avoid placing plants directly under vents
- Rotate plants to prevent leaning or stress

Environment

- Increase airflow gently (not directly on plants)
- Be mindful of heaters and AC units
- Watch for dry air, especially in winter

Routine checks

- Look under leaves occasionally
- Check soil moisture before watering
- Notice changes early

When Protection Helps — and When It Hurts

Protection helps when:

- Plants are newly planted
- Damage is consistent
- Environmental stress is ongoing

Protection may hurt when:

- Plants are over-covered
- Airflow is restricted
- Stress increases from constant handling

Sometimes less intervention leads to stronger plants.

Big Sis Reminder

You don't have to protect plants from everything — just enough to give them a fair chance.

Resource 22: Seasonal Care Adjustments at a Glance

(Referenced in Chapter 12)

***This guide reflects general seasonal patterns for many common container plants. Always consider your specific plant type, growing method, and local conditions.

Plants adjust their pace with the seasons. This guide helps you know what to change — and what to leave alone as the year shifts.

Spring

Many plants begin active growth as light increases.

- Water needs often rise gradually
- New growth may appear
- Light improves naturally
- Gentle feeding may resume if growth is active

Focus: waking up, not rushing

Summer

Many warm-season plants grow most actively.

- Watering needs often increase
- Heat stress may occur
- Containers dry out faster
- Extra protection may be needed

Focus: consistency and protection

Fall

Some plants continue growing, while others slow down.

- Growth may taper or shift
- Watering needs often decrease
- Feeding is usually reduced
- Observation becomes more important

Focus: adjustment, not assumptions

Winter

Many plants enter rest, especially indoors.

- Growth often slows or pauses
- Light is reduced
- Soil stays wet longer
- Feeding is usually unnecessary

Focus: rest and patience

Big Sis Reminder

Seasons guide plants — but plants still have individual needs.

Resource 23: When to Adjust vs When to Leave Plants Alone

(Referenced in Chapter 12)

Not every change needs fixing. This guide helps you decide when action helps — and when waiting is wiser.

You can usually wait if:

- Growth is slower but steady
- Leaves look healthy
- The season just changed
- Light levels dropped naturally

You may want to adjust if:

- Leaves are consistently yellowing
- Soil stays wet for long periods
- Plants are stressed by heat or cold
- Conditions changed suddenly

Common Helpful Adjustments

- Water less often
- Improve airflow
- Move plants slightly for light
- Pause feeding

Big Sis Reminder

Sometimes the best care is giving plants space to adjust on their own.

www.ingramcontent.com/pod-product-compliance
Lightning Source LLC
Chambersburg PA
CBHW040250090526
44586CB00040B/2634